MARY MORRIS

ALL THE WAY TO THE TIGERS

Mary Morris is the author of numerous works of fiction, including the novels *Gateway to the Moon*, *The Jazz Palace*, *A Mother's Love*, and *House Arrest*, and of nonfiction, including the classic *Nothing to Declare: Memoirs of a Woman Traveling Alone*. She is a recipient of the Rome Fellowship in Literature and the 2016 Anisfield-Wolf Book Award for Fiction. She lives in Brooklyn, New York.

"The author of the classic travelogue *Nothing to Declare* this time ventures to Pench, India, in part to glimpse the apex predator she's long dreamed of, in part to prove that a recent injury won't end the habit of far-flung travel that has nourished her for six decades. The resulting memoir—wry and wistful—reveals a woman finally comfortable with her own imperfections and, when she gets the chance, unafraid to look a tiger in the eye." —*O, The Oprah Magazine*

"A travel narrative in the tradition of Cheryl Strayed and Elizabeth Gilbert." —Read It Forward

"Morris is frank, funny, and incisive as she revisits her 'free-ranging' Chicago childhood, single motherhood, and her start as writer, and expounds on tigers in the world and in the imagination. . . . Morris's epigrammatic memoir is a finely wrought mosaic of unexpected and provocative pieces cunningly fit together." —*Booklist*

"Engrossing. . . . Morris's descriptions of remote beauty, grinding urban poverty, and exotic adventures will captivate armchair tourists and travel memoir fans." —*Publishers Weekly*

"Honest, observant, and striking." —*Kirkus Reviews*

ALL THE WAY
TO THE TIGERS

{ *A Memoir* }

MARY MORRIS

ANCHOR BOOKS

A Division of Penguin Random House LLC

New York

To Kate and Chris
And to wild things everywhere

FIRST ANCHOR BOOKS EDITION, MAY 2021

Copyright © 2020 by Mary Morris

All rights reserved. Published in the United States by
Anchor Books, a division of Penguin Random House LLC,
New York, and distributed in Canada by Penguin Random House
Canada Limited, Toronto. Originally published in hardcover
in the United States by Nan A. Talese, a division of
Penguin Random House LLC, New York, in 2020.

Anchor Books and colophon are registered trademarks of
Penguin Random House LLC.

The Library of Congress has cataloged the
Nan A. Talese edition as follows:
Names: Morris, Mary, author.
Title: All the way to the tigers : a memoir / by Mary Morris.
Description: First edition. | New York : Nan A. Talese, 2020.
Identifiers: LCCN 2019026131 (print) | LCCN 2019026132 (ebook)
Subjects: LCSH: India—Description and travel. | Safaris—India.
| Morris, Mary, 1947– —Travel—India. | Novelists, American—
20th century—Biography. | Tiger—India—Anecdotes. | Women
travelers—Biography. | New York (N.Y.)—Biography.
Classification: LCC DS414.2 .M675 2020 (print) |
LCC DS414.2 (ebook) | DDC 915.404/532092 B—dc23
LC record available at https://lccn.loc.gov/2019026131

Anchor Books Trade Paperback ISBN: 978-0-593-08102-0
eBook ISBN: 978-0-385-54610-2

Book design by Maggie Hinders

www.anchorbooks.com

Printed in the United States of America

He would go on a journey. Not far.
Not all the way to the tigers.

THOMAS MANN, *Death in Venice*

ALL THE WAY

TO THE TIGERS

1

India, 2011

WE HAVEN'T MOVED in what seems like hours. It's late afternoon in January, and I can see my breath. Our jeep is at a crossroads where my driver and guide sit in silence. Ajay is listening. His eyes dart, skimming the woods. But mainly he listens. I'm listening too. Though I'm not sure what I'm supposed to hear. I've got two horsehair blankets across my legs, a hot-water bottle cooling in my lap, and a scarf wrapped around my head. I'm shivering, not only from the cold but also perhaps from a fever, and coughing from a virus that's sunk deep into my chest. As the sun is going down, a family of langur monkeys gathers in the trees.

Something rustles the bush, and there's chatter above. A bird with turquoise-and-black feathers that look like an evening gown flits through the forest. Another with two long purple plumes perches on a low-hanging branch.

Ajay points to the scat of an elephant in the road, but it's a tame elephant, one of four used by the rangers to patrol these woods. A jackal bursts from the brush and crosses our path. But the tiger eludes us. It is the tiger everyone comes to see. Not the snake-eating hawk, the spotted deer, the wild boar. It's all about the tiger.

Sudhir, our driver, wants to push on, but Ajay motions for him to be patient. Ajay is still listening. It is almost dusk. The other jeeps have called it a day. In fact there were very few. I've seen almost no tourists. I am alone with my driver and guide in this jeep that holds eight. It's getting colder, almost freezing as the darkness settles in. I am in the jungle, sick and cold, with blankets wrapped around my thighs, searching for tigers. We've been out for days without a sign, but Ajay and Sudhir want to persist. It has become a point of pride. I've seen beautiful birds, I tell them. White-spotted and sambar deer. I've seen a jackal race down the road and monkeys, mocking us from trees. I don't need to see more. But it seems that I am the one thing in this jungle that they won't listen to. Slowly Ajay raises his hand. He's whispering to Sudhir. He listens, then points, and now both men are pointing in different directions. "What is it?" I ask. As always I hear nothing.

"Sambar deer alarm call. She is warning spotted deer."

Suddenly we are off as Sudhir zigzags along the twists and turns of the rutted dirt road. I bump up and down in the back, holding the frame as we approach a fork. "Go right, go right," Ajay mouths, his hand waving Sudhir on.

We race down into a big meadow surrounded by trees. Once more we stop and the men stand up. Ajay borrows my binoculars. He scans the meadow, focused on some movement in the brush. "In there," Ajay says. "She's somewhere in there." Ajay explains that all unseen tigers are referred to as "she." The tiger, hidden in the brush, is always she.

We wait for her to move while we stand still. There's an eerie quiet in the air as we sit, watching. Using my hand as a visor, my eyes scan the woods as well. She's out there. I have no doubt. My guide knows too. We are silent and the jungle around us is quiet as we wait for the bushes to rustle and the tiger to emerge. She's crouching in the tall grass that hides her stripes. But I'm willing to wait. In my own way I've been waiting for a long time.

2

Brooklyn, 2008

ON A WINTER MORNING I turn to my husband over coffee. "Let's go skating," I say. It is a clear, crisp day—the beginning of an eight-month sabbatical that I've been looking forward to for a long time. My calendar is empty of obligations—devoid of anything except the words JURY DUTY. It is jury duty that preoccupies me that morning. I received a summons the week before and I am obsessed with it. What if I'm put on a case? I fear being tied down. Otherwise nothing stands between me and months during which I can do whatever I choose.

I've spent seven years waiting for this sabbatical. Given that we change all the cells in our bodies every seven years, I am a different person than I was the last time I had a leave. And this is my first leave in more than twenty years when I don't have a child at home. I'm looking forward to months of free time and travel. On sheets of paper I've written wish lists of the things I plan to do, places I'd see.

We are going to Rome, where Larry will run in the Rome Marathon and I'll take a watercolor class—something I've always wanted to do. Then on to a house swap in Spain. Our daughter, Kate, who is spending the year in Ireland, is going to join us for her spring break. Then we'll travel to Morocco. Soon we'll be taking a ferry across the Strait of Gibraltar. These journeys are my lifeblood. And at times they are also my livelihood. I'm contemplating a year of nomadic roaming. I have things to do. Adventures await. Time lies before me like an open road, and I want to begin by going skating with my husband.

"Sure," Larry replies, seeing how eager I am, "let's go."

Ice-skating is something I've done all my life. I grew up on skates and skated as an adult for years. Childhood friends of mine—brother and sister twins—competed at the national level in pairs and I loved watching them practice at our rink. I have fantasies of my own. I love zipping

around as the three tenors croon or the theme song from
The Lion King soars. Larry, a Canadian, is also an excellent
skater. We skate apart and together. We waltz on blades.
People admire our dance steps.

But I have no business skating that day. The previous
year a back injury kept me off the ice. Last May I had surgery for a ruptured disk. Now, with my newfound freedom, I'm eager to return. Yet despite all the stretching and
swimming I do, my back is still stiff from that injury, but
I want to go. So I pop four Motrin and I'm off. Isn't that
what real athletes do?

As I'm lacing up, one seasoned skater pauses as she's
leaving to tell me to be careful. "The ice is hard," she says.
I'm not sure what "hard" ice means. It seems redundant.
Isn't ice always hard? But when I get out, I understand.
The ice is so solid that my blades only graze the surface. I
can't get a grip. Still, for almost an hour Larry and I zoom
along. It feels so good to be back and, though I am a little
rusty, I can still do most of my moves. Front crossovers,
back crossovers. We even waltz for a song or two. Then
we skate apart again. I'm just getting into a groove when
Larry whizzes by, pointing to an imaginary watch on his
wrist. "Time to go," he says.

But I want to skate a little longer. I hold up my fingers.
"Just five more minutes," I mouth. It's a moment I've gone
back to many times.

3

I ALWAYS want to stay longer than I should. Like some-one who is compulsively late, except I am the opposite. I linger. At a party I'm the last to leave. On a morning walk I stall. I'll stare at a bird in flight, sunlight flickering on a lake long after my husband or dog have moved on. I keep people on the phone until they tell me they have to go. I stay at the movie until the final credits roll. Perhaps because I grew up with an impatient father. A man who always had to arrive early and leave before anyone else. He hated traffic jams, delays. Anything that took him out of his way. Anyplace where he might get lost. As a child, I missed the end of movies, the curtain calls at a show. There was never a detour for ice cream.

Every spring we went to the circus, but my father made us leave before the last act. He couldn't take the departing crowds. And the last act was always the big cats. As the cage was being set up, my father stood. "Let's go." Though we pleaded, he wouldn't relent. I never got to watch the lions, the tigers, the green-eyed panthers growling from their pedestals, leaping through flaming hoops. Before the first crack of the whip, we were gone.

4

AS A CHILD I had a tiger dream. I had it often, and it was always the same. There is a tiger at the foot of my bed. He sits on his haunches, sharpening his claws on my bedposts. I stare at him. His claws extended, focused on his task. He is never in a hurry. His amber eyes are on me. When his claws are sharp, he gets into a crouch as tigers do. And then he pounces. He springs through the air and just before he lands on top of me, I wake up. Years later I learned that you cannot dream your own death. But it never occurred to me that the tiger meant to kill me. He had something else in mind.

5

India, 2011

THE MINUTE I arrive in Delhi, I know I've packed the wrong clothes. I thought I was heading into some warm, tropical zone. But it seems not. My friend Susan, who'd been to India the previous winter, warned me. She went to Rajasthan and told me that she was freezing. "Bring layers. Bring warmer clothes than you think you will need. A sweatshirt, a fleece jacket. And bring a hot-water bottle. You won't be sorry." But I would be much farther south than Rajasthan in a more temperate zone, so I didn't pay too much attention to this. Still, at the last minute I tossed the hot-water bottle into my bag, and I'm grateful that I did.

It is freezing here. As cold as New York except for one major difference: The houses don't have heat. All I have that's got any warmth are a sweatshirt, a light sweater, and a cloth jacket. Even the layers won't be enough. I arrive at the guesthouse where I'll be staying. It's about one in the morning, and it is no warmer inside than it is outside.

Despite the late hour Charlotte, her husband, and Juli greet me. Juli, a small, thin girl with a wide smile and bright, dark eyes, places a garland of marigolds around my neck, then hands me a glass of guava juice. The juice is sweet and from a can, but it tastes surprisingly good. I am exhausted as I go into my room, where it is still very cold. Charlotte apologizes. "We were going to buy a space heater but we didn't get around to it today."

"It is chilly." I am wishing I had a space heater. Also I don't want to admit this, but I'm not feeling very well. My throat is raw and there's a sore blistering in my mouth—a bad sign for me. I am hoping that a good night's sleep will make me feel better, but I sleep only two hours, as if I've had a good solid nap. I am clearly not on Delhi time. I go out of my room in search of some water to drink. There, on a small cot, I see the child, curled under a blanket near the stove. Fast asleep.

I had assumed that Juli was a relative or granddaughter of the family, but it turns out that she is an orphan girl who has been loaned by the nuns. There is apparently an orphanage nearby and they let some of the children work in households. In exchange the children are given lessons. Over tea just after dawn Charlotte explains that Juli's only real chance is to pass a national exam, which will admit her to private school. Otherwise her life will probably be lived on the street. She says this casually, as if she's asking me to pass the milk.

Just after seven I shower and get dressed. An old friend of mine, Catherine, who has been working on a Fulbright in Hyderabad, is flying up to Delhi to spend the day with me. I am struck at the odd synchronicity. It was Catherine I met when my journeys began in Mexico three decades ago, and now it is Catherine who will briefly be my guide again. She's taken an early flight and will meet me at Charlotte's guesthouse by ten. She has a driver and guide arranged. In vintage Catherine fashion it's all been taken care of, and I'm fine to just go with the flow.

Catherine and I met at the pool of Hotel Quinta Loreto in San Miguel de Allende. She was swimming an interminable mile in the tiny pool, and when she was done, I asked if I could borrow her goggles. We've been friends ever since. For years we traveled all over Latin America together. When I told her I was on my way to India, she told me she'd be in India! "I'll meet you anywhere," she said. We haven't seen each other in a few years.

Now it is January 2011—almost three years to the day of our last meeting. She looks good. Strong and youthful.

The car she hired is waiting to take us around. Catherine has our itinerary all mapped out.

It's rush hour in Delhi. We move at a snail's pace. We pass people living in cardboard boxes on the median strip. On that same strip laundry hangs to dry on electric cables. People live on the sidewalks, beneath their fruit stands, in their rickshaws. Last year a drunk Bollywood star ran over a family of four who lived beside their cart, killing them all. In the rubble of a building that crashed to the ground, former residents huddle before a small fire. We pass a butcher shop, a chicken store, a fish market in tin shacks with no refrigeration. A woman zips by on a moped wearing a fringed lampshade as a helmet. We pass a winter "steal" market where you can buy hubcaps, sockets, spark plugs, tires, ball bearings, vinyl seats, steering wheels—all from stolen cars.

Misery is etched on faces. A man peers out from the blackest of holes. A young girl with brown bulging eyes, her skull wrapped entirely in gauze, makes eye contact with me as we pass. She has the blank stare of someone already leaving this world. Then she is lost behind a sign that reads "Don't Urinate or Defecate in Public." A clinical lab offers the analysis of blood, urine, stool, semen, and sputum. Live chickens and monkeys, all tied together by their feet, float on bicycle handles past the Presidential Palace. Crazed, starving dogs too lazy to beg lie down across the streets except for a lucky one that sits on the sidewalk, fat, in a pink wool coat, a collar around its neck. Pigeons shit all over a new Hyundai.

I cannot take my eyes off this pulsing, mad city as we whirl through. Just before lunch I am coaxed into sitting on the ground beside a snake charmer and his hooded cobra. I am hesitant, but our guide reassures me. "It has no fangs." So I sit as the cobra rises and twists and stares at me, just inches from my face, while Catherine laughs her head off, snapping pictures, and the snake charmer plays his melancholy tune. Later I will learn that you can't actually defang a cobra because that will kill it, but you can milk it and hope that its venom hasn't come back by the time you're sitting next to it.

At lunch I tell Catherine about my trip. "Tigers?" Catherine asks, digging into her curry. I tell her about my plan to find tigers. She nods thoughtfully. "How exciting. Are you going to Rajasthan?" Rajasthan is where most tourists go to see tigers, but I was very specific with the agent who helped arrange my trip. I didn't want to go to the Golden Triangle. Not Rajasthan, not Jaipur, no Taj Mahal. I wanted to be off the tourist trail. But as I explain my purpose, a flicker of worry passes across Catherine's face. "Well, good luck."

Near the end of the day I am coughing. "You want some cough drops?" Catherine asks and I take a cherry-coated something that feels gooey in my mouth. "You don't look so well," she says, not bothering to hide her concern.

I nod. "I'm not feeling great." I run my tongue over the

blister that has begun to blossom on my inside lip. I harbor a secret virus that seems to live in my lower lip. When I get too stressed or run-down, it pulsates. Just before I get sick, it erupts. Doctors don't believe me, but I know it's there. It's not really contagious—at least it doesn't seem to be. No one in my family has ever gotten this. It's my own private virus—one that mutated into its present form just for me. And once it's revived, I dread the aftermath. I'm hoping against hope that some rest will make it go away, but I'm not really sure where that rest will be coming from.

It's evening as Catherine, with great fanfare, drops me off at Charlotte's guesthouse. We say our goodbyes with air-kisses, given that I think I'm coming down with something. "Let me know how it goes," Catherine calls as she slips back into her cab.

When I get in, I am exhausted. All I want to do is sleep, but I am also hungry. Charlotte, who is busy on her laptop, tells me that there is a good restaurant nearby just across the main street. "I'll walk you there," she says.

We make our way down a dark street until we reach an intersection. Before me stretches a four-lane road that seems to have more like a dozen lanes. On it is a hodge-podge of cyclists, cars, trucks, scooters, rickshaws moving in a clatter of horns. Endless beeping, honking, shouting. Charlotte points across the street. "Over there," she says. I see a bunch of stands and shops and one that seems to be a restaurant. "The food is good." And she leaves me.

At first, I do what I've learned in the Western world. I wait for the light. But when it turns, no one seems to notice that it's even there. In fact, there is no perceptible change. I step out, stick my toe in, but nothing interrupts this flow that has no beginning and no end. I stand like a nonswimmer before the sea. The green light comes and goes, then comes again, and I still make no progress. I decide to try and do what the natives do. I watch an Indian man as he makes his way across. A scooter just misses him. A taxi slams on its horn. He holds his hand out. Some cars seem to slow down. Sort of. Or weave around him. One or two stop. And my hero makes it to the other side.

But I have yet to move. Hungry and thwarted, I stand befuddled at the corner of Madness and Chaos like a math student before an impossible problem. I have no idea how to cross this road. I can't bear the humiliation of arriving in India and dying on my way to eat a bowl of curry. At last, defeated, I head back to the guesthouse. Charlotte looks at me, surprised. "That was very fast," she says.

"I didn't get there," I tell her. "I couldn't figure out how to cross the street."

Charlotte nods. "Oh, I know. It is almost impossible. I never let my son go there." I want to ask why she let me, but I don't. There must be some logic operating here, but I can't grasp it.

"I'm still hungry," I tell her.

"Oh, well, you could order in. They have takeout."

"They do?" I wish I'd known this an hour ago, but no

matter. We place the call. I order a vegetable curry that arrives in ten minutes. I sit at the dining-room table, eating alone except for Juli lying on her little cot, her eyes open, watching me. I want to ask her if she is hungry, but it isn't hunger I see in her round, dark eyes.

Two-thirty a.m. and I'm still wide-awake.

6

Brooklyn, 2008

THE THREE TURN is a fairly simple maneuver. It consists of a pivot in which you shift your weight on one skate and reverse the direction in which you are skating. Your hip and shoulder must turn at the same time. The trick is to do it at speed on ice. It is this turn that enables a figure skater to go from forward to backward, inside blade to outside blade, right to left. There are eight separate three turns and, for the kind of skating I enjoyed, I should have mastered at least one of them by now. I spent years trying, but I hadn't really improved. I'm too tentative. Afraid to put my whole body into it. I've been struggling for some time while I watch others, including my husband, do it effortlessly.

Off to the side two fellow skaters are practicing theirs. Left, inside, forward. Right, outside, backward. They are women whose skating I've admired over the years. They move so gracefully. It just looks like a matter of confidence. Watching as they shift from forward to back, then forward again, I want to try mine as well. I just have to put my whole body into it. Don't hesitate. I have a feeling this is the winter when I'll master it.

I skate over to the boards, ignoring my stiffening back. Or Larry, who is anxious to leave. He has to get to work. As I prepare for my turn, he gives me that signal again. "Two minutes," I shout. He smiles and gives me a shrug. He's used to my stalling tactics. He does what any parent in a similar situation would do. He pretends he's leaving. I want to give the three turn a couple of tries. No more than that. Unless I want to get home on my own, I have to leave soon.

I stand straight, arms out to the side. I begin my pivot, but I lack momentum—and perhaps the confidence—to complete it. I barely make it around at all and just glide back against the boards. I want one more try. I feel sure I can get it if I push off harder than I have before. I give myself a greater shove, but my blade doesn't seem to hold the ice. As that skater warned me earlier, the ice is hard. Now I really know what she means.

My foot spins out from under me like a quarter, twirling on the ground. I go down and hit the ice. The pain is excruciating as I sit, stunned, clutching my ankle.

"Are you all right?" A man comes to a halt beside me. I grimace as I tell him I am. I want to be. Larry, who is just leaving the ice, skates back to me, a look of concern on his face.

"It's nothing," I tell them, waving everyone away. "I'm fine." I refuse the ambulance that the rink guards offer. (Later, when I learn that Natasha Richardson refused an ambulance before she died from a minor skiing fall, I understand how easily such a decision can be made. *I'm all right. There's nothing wrong with me.*)

I've never broken a bone before. Why would I suddenly now? I'm not going to waste an afternoon in the emergency room for a sprain. I have things to do. I have plans. Never mind that my foot doesn't seem to be fitting well into my ankle joint. I can't really feel my foot at all. I used to joke that I don't have time to move, get divorced, or die. I'm too busy for any of those things. I added going to the hospital to that list.

My husband and the other man each give me a shoulder as they cart me off the ice, the way linebackers tote a fellow player with a crushed patella. A woman with a thick Russian accent, all bundled up, skates over. She tells me that I should go home and chop up onions, add hot pepper, pour vodka over the concoction, put it all into a sock, and wear the thing to bed, and in the morning I'll be ready to dance.

I thank the Russian woman for her advice as my husband removes my skate. There is a shot of pain, but then it subsides. I feel better out of the boot. Two skate guards help me to the car. "Are you sure you don't want to go to the hospital?" one of them asks. I'm sure, I tell them as they cart me across the parking lot. In the car home I'm thinking about chopping onions.

Larry parks as close as he can to the house, but I have to hop over the curb, then crawl up our front steps. Inside, I rest in the blue chair by the window with my foot raised. Larry packs my ankle in ice. But after an hour it's clear that something is wrong. Now the pain is terrible and the swelling is getting worse. And my skin is turning very red. I need to get to the hospital. I need an X-ray. Larry phones his office to say he'll be in later that day and helps me to the door.

I make it out of the house, but something happens at the top of our front steps. I lose my balance. I try to grab Larry's arm, but my other leg goes out from beneath me. So I fall again, striking my injured ankle on the concrete steps on my way down. I watch as my foot twists in a direction that I don't think is possible. And frankly, it's not.

As Larry dials 911, I scream the way I've only heard people scream in horror films. I didn't know that my vocal cords could make a sound as piercing as that. Half the neighborhood races out of their houses and stands in front of ours, gaping, not knowing what to do while my pain-racked brain waves them away.

As I listen to the sound of an ambulance and the rescue squad approaching, I find myself thinking about giraffes. I saw a documentary about them once. A collapsed giraffe never rises again. Once the legs go out from under him, a giraffe's life is done. I'm pondering this as an NYFD rescue squad member is cutting off the candy-cane Christmas socks my daughter gave me. "I'll be all right, won't I?" I ask him.

"Ma'am," the fireman says, staring at my shattered ankle, "you're in shock."

7

IN A RECENT POLL tigers are shown to be the most popular animals in the world—followed by dogs, horses, cats. Tigers are, so to speak, in our blood. But what makes us think that there is actual power to be had in tiger blood? In his rants Charlie Sheen said that tiger blood runs in his veins. Noted zoologists will counter by saying that tiger blood is the same as ours. Still, there is now a hashtag for #TigerBlood. And some of us can remember Tony the Tiger on the Frosted Flakes package; he was supposed to give us power to start the day. Or when we used to be able to gas up by putting a tiger in our tanks. In fact, the word "Viagra" derives from the Sanskrit word meaning tiger.

In the most northern reserves of India tigers no longer roam. Their torsos are found with their paws, head, and testicles chopped off. They have been poached, their carcasses carted through Tibet into China, where the Chinese believe they will grow potent from tiger testicles and tiger marrow. They want to consume the tiger down to its very bones.

8

India, 2011

AT FOUR IN THE MORNING a car comes to get me. I am flying from Delhi to Nagpur, where another car will meet me, this time to take me to the Pench Tiger Reserve. I'm heading south to the middle of Madhya Pradesh and two tiger reserves. At the airport I'm getting my travel legs back. Before going through security, I note the list of unauthorized carry-on items: knives, guns, ammunition, cricket bat, hockey stick, pepper spray, jar of pickles. Jar of pickles? Perhaps it is the intensity of the spice that makes it a threat. Why not other jars? Or is "pickles" generic for all condiments?

Perhaps it is the Indian equivalent of snow globes— which can no longer be carried on board planes in the United States. Snow globes as weapons of war. It is hard to comprehend. At any rate, I am relieved that no pickle jars will be traveling with me. Though in my checked bags, a sign informs me, I can carry dry ice, a mercury barometer, and a camping stove.

The sun is rising over India. I am tired and hungry, having forgotten to eat before leaving. I am also trying to ignore the fact that my throat seems worse and so is my cough. Still, I'm excited to be on my way at last, looking for tigers. On the two-hour flight I don't sleep or even read. I stare out the window all the way.

In the waiting area in Nagpur I am immediately greeted by a young man who says to me, "Hello, Miss Morris." Since there are a lot of people milling about, I ask him how he knew it was me. He said, "Oh, I was just looking for a woman who was about the same age as my mother." I guess that's what I get for asking, but I wouldn't have minded a more gracious reply.

This young man is only here to meet me at the airport. It is my driver who will take me where I need to go. But first we must have some chai. The young man takes me out into the street, where men stand before a boiling cauldron of milky tea. "It's fine," the young man says. "You can drink this." I suppose he wouldn't bring his mother here if he didn't think it was all right, and, after all, the tea is boiling. I take a cup in my hands. It is hot and sweet and delicious. As I'm sipping it, a car pulls up.

"So you've come to look for tigers" are the first words my driver, Dinesh, says. He's a handsome and fit middle-aged man in an impeccably clean white shirt and a spotless car.

"Yes, I'm hoping to." He gives an odd little nod that is hard to interpret but I don't think I'm the first person he's driven who has this goal in mind.

"Oh, you will. You will. I can promise you." As Dinesh is putting my bag into the trunk, he motions for me to get in. I'm not sure whether I am expected to sit in the front or the back. For Dinesh it is whatever I want, but he has a bottle of cold water, hand towelettes, and Kleenex waiting for me in the back. I climb in and already I'm coughing and sneezing. I apologize and tell him that I believe it is a sinus problem (from which I've suffered for years) and I am not infectious. I half believe this. I have had upper respiratory infections before, but I'm not a doctor and really I have no idea. I am only hoping it is true.

Before leaving Nagpur, Dinesh wants to take me on a short sightseeing tour. Something I don't really want to do, but there are some army barracks he wants to show me, and a temple. Then he takes me to a strange spot. It is the exact geographical center of India. Zero mile. It was declared so in 1847. For a few moments I stand before a pillar of stone and four rearing horses. It is sort of an intriguing thought that I am standing in the dead center of this large, fraught, complex nation. And clearly Dinesh is proud to show this to me.

After viewing the navel of India, I decide to sit in the front seat. It is a long drive and I don't feel very comfortable being chauffeured. Also I can barely hear what he has to say. I crawl into the front. On the dashboard is the photograph of a handsome boy. "Is that your son?" I ask and Dinesh nods in that Indian way where it is hard to tell if they are saying yes or no or maybe.

"Yes, he is my son."

"Well, he's a handsome boy," I tell him, trying to make conversation. "I have a daughter."

"Just one?" Dinesh holds up one finger.

"Yes, that's plenty." I laugh, but he doesn't.

· · ·

We set out along the road to Pench. A long, chaotic industrial strip, filled with tire outlets, packs of wild dogs, sacred cows, feral pigs devouring trash. Women in bright-colored saris balance water jugs on their heads. Girls on mopeds, their heads and faces completely covered, dark glasses on, zip by. Women crouch, weaving garlands of flowers.

We drive through towns packed with marketplaces, teeming with rickshaws. From beneath piles of tires men peer. Cows walk down the main highway. India is a good place to be a cow. They are everywhere. In the middle of roads, lying down on median strips. They are sacred to the Hindus, who, despite the fact that many humans are literally starving, will never eat them. The sacredness of the Indian cow, however, comes more or less from the same place as the celibacy of priests. That is, a practical rather than spiritual one. In the case of priests it was decided that descendants would present a problem when it came to the division of church property. In a similar way the number of cows Indians once possessed represented wealth and power. Only afterward did the divine enter into these concerns and cows became more matters of faith than real estate. Lord Shiva never sanctified cows. Regardless, they roam freely and Dinesh is careful not to hit one on the road.

A highway sign reads "Danger Creeps While Safety

Sleeps." We cross the Kanhan River, passing thatched-roof villages. All along this road more highways are being built. Trucks dump gravel, others haul rocks, all with the name Backbone Enterprises. It seems to me the perfect name for all of India. It is this expansion of roads that impinges the most on the tiger's habitat, and I can see why. Everywhere I look there is nothing but miles and miles of roads. And more are being built every day.

We pass a school where a line of children stand in the yard, tugging on their own ears. "Why are they doing that?" I ask Dinesh, who tells me that these are children who haven't done their homework and they are being punished and are on public display. "It doesn't hurt them," he says, "it just embarrasses them."

Once more I ask about his son, whom he tells me is in boarding school. "Boarding school. Isn't that a little unusual?"

And then Dinesh's whole sad story unfolds.

Not long after their son was born, his young wife had a brain hemorrhage. She had surgery and was better, but then she hemorrhaged again. Another surgery, but when it happened the third time she refused the surgery, and she died. Obviously this was tragic, but then the story gets a little murky. There was some problem with Dinesh's in-laws, who tried to take his son away. They took Dinesh to court. They sued for custody and lost. Since then Dinesh has never spoken to them. And his son has never seen them.

"So your son doesn't see his grandparents?" Dinesh shakes his head. "Or his aunts, uncles? His cousins?" Again Dinesh proudly shakes his head.

"But who cares for him while you are on the road?"

"Oh," he tells me, eyes on the road, "there is a woman who takes care of him when he's not in school." I am saddened at the thought of Dinesh's lonely boy and I am also feeling weak. I am feverish and I've wrapped a scarf around my throat, but still I am coughing. "You need some medicine," he tells me. "I will stop for you." Dinesh seems to know everywhere to stop—for a bite, for cough drops. And he is an expert on bathrooms. He knows where all the clean bathrooms are. Something I'll come to appreciate in the several days in which we are thrown together.

We drive along until we come to a town, where Dinesh pulls to the side of the road. He races in and returns with a bag filled with cough drops and a small flask of whiskey. "This is for your throat," he says. Who am I to argue?

Driving on, we come to another village, and I ask Dinesh if we can stop. He nods his head back and forth, but I can't really tell if it means yes, no, or maybe. But then it seems to me as if perhaps everything in India means "maybe." He pulls over, so I assume it's all right. But then I am uncomfortable. I don't want to embarrass the villagers, but Dinesh assures me it won't. "They will be happy for your visit."

I bring my camera. In the village on a front porch we are greeted by a very old woman who has no teeth.

The woman hollers something, and a man appears—also old and toothless. I am smiling at them and they look at me askance. Dinesh gives them the traditional greeting, putting his hands together, and says, "Namaste," which means basically "go in peace." A young girl appears with a pitcher and some water for us to drink.

I am hesitant but Dinesh takes a ceramic cup from her hands and a long drink. I feel bad about not accepting the water, but I am determined not to get sicker than I already am. In the car as we push on, Dinesh tells me not to smile at people in greeting. "If you smile at them, they think you are making fun of them." From then on I will greet people only with my hands pressed together, bowing, and say, "Namaste."

As we get closer to Pench the road is lined with red-faced rhesus macaque monkeys. They are everywhere and it doesn't surprise me to learn that they are the least endangered primates in the world. These are the monkeys used in laboratories, to test the latest cancer drug or eye shadow. They have weirdly human faces—due in part to the fact that their faces are hairless. They stand on their hind legs by the side of the road, palms outstretched, begging for food. I think they are cute and want to take their picture until Dinesh tells me that they have left the jungle and come to the road because they are starving.

9

THE TIGER. Elusive, mysterious, hidden, hiding. You cannot make friends with the tiger, Pi's father tells him in *Life of Pi*. It reminds me of a story a friend told me—though it sounds like an urban legend. An acquaintance of hers had a pet boa constrictor. The woman was in a lonely patch in her life so she began bringing the snake to bed with her. After a few weeks her snake stopped eating. Not even live mice could entice it. She took it to the vet, who could find nothing wrong with the boa and asked if she was in any way being intimate with her snake, and the woman confessed that she did let it sleep with her in her bed. "It's getting ready to eat you," the vet told her.

10

WE ARE ONLY seven meals away from anarchy. My veterinarian told me that. We were speaking about predators in general and he told me that if humans went without food for more than two days, we'd start killing one another with baseball bats. "You can imagine how desperate an animal can become if you take away its food."

11

EXCEPT FOR animals that live in the dark recesses of the sea, tigers are one of the most elusive creatures on earth. They are apex predators, killing machines. Ambush hunters. They will watch their game for hours and sometimes days before they pounce, always striking from the back or the side. Their retractable claws can slice through any flesh. Tigers have no natural enemies, but they fear anything white. White does not appear in their dense jungle world. White is emptiness, blankness. They have no camouflage against it.

When the maharajas wanted to go hunting, they had their servants weave white sheets through the tiger's terrain, flushing her out. And when the tiger ran away from all that whiteness, the maharaja shot her.

12

I HAVE ALWAYS had an interest in beginnings. The beginning of friendships, of romances, of books, of plays. Origin stories. The blank page. If I come in late to a movie, even if it's just the credits rolling, I never recover. I must start from scratch. I go back to a March day. I know it is March because my father is preparing his taxes. At least that is what I've been told he is doing. And because it is rainy and gray and the garden, my mother's garden, has yet to bloom. In fact all I see is mud. It is a miserable Sunday and my mother says to me that I can play in the den, but I can't disturb my father.

My father was a methodical, orderly man, especially with his business affairs, a trait I have tried to emulate without much success. There was also a much darker, more complicated side to him, but that is not what this anecdote is about. On this March day my father sits at a card table in his yellow cashmere sweater and brown slippers. The table is covered with slips of paper, all neatly stacked, thick pads of yellow paper, and pencils, sharpened to a fine point. He has his big, wide checkbook open before him.

"You can play in there," my mother says, "but don't bother him." Of course if I go into the den, I am going to bother him. I have nothing to do. The den has sliding doors and I like sliding them back and forth. I can do this hundreds of times in an hour. Another thing I like is to sit on the couch that looks out onto the garden and blow my breath on the glass, then scribble on it. I do not know how to write. I do not know how to read. I am four years old and bored.

My father tries to shoo me away, telling me to go and play. Or watch TV. But I refuse to leave his side. For lack of anything better to do with me, he writes my name across the top of a lined yellow pad. MARY. There, he says, that's your name. Now: "You write it."

Of course, he knows I can't. I don't know how to write. But it is a good distraction for half an hour, if that. I'm often surprised at how I recall this day with perfect precision. Its grayness. My father's somber, serious face. His yellow sweater and brown shoes. The yellow pad and its stripes and MARY written across the top. I am given a pencil and sent to the floor, where I try to do what my father has shown me.

I clasp the pencil like a dagger. The way a woman about to commit a crime of passion might hold a knife—by its handle, a weapon, ready to plunge. I have not yet learned the delicacy of holding a pencil as one holds chopsticks between thumb and index finger. Certainly I cannot write in what will become my clear, loping script.

Also it seems that I am left-handed. My father cannot show me how to hold the pencil or the proper slant of the pad. (In fact, for my whole life I will turn the page almost upside down. Once a flight attendant knelt down beside and asked me, "Can you really write like that?") I struggle. Even to this day I can see the letters forming one after the other. I try over and over until I believe that I have correctly copied my name. I know that my father will be pleased as I present it to him. My nose just reaches to the table as I push the pad back onto the card table. I am proud of what I have done. I am on my tiptoes. And I see it now, as if it is the hand of God, my father's finger coming down. "The R is backward," he says.

The R is backward. My father's harsh words. I have certainly heard worse critiques of my work in the ensuing years, but that one has reverberated for decades. It is the critique that made me want to persevere, to never give up. I want to get it right, no matter what it takes. My first revision. I go back on the floor, pencil in hand, and begin again.

13

CUBS ARE PRIME TARGETS for predators, including their own fathers.

14

IT'S 1967 and my father gives me my first journal. I am about to depart for France for my junior year abroad—a year during which he will never visit me. Before I sail, he gives me a soft green leather book with gold trim on the pages and my name embossed in gold on the cover. What makes my father do this I'll never know. He hated the fact that I was leaving, and that I had in some way already left. He had never encouraged me to write before. Yet he gives me this book.

In it he inscribes: "This book with its blank pages is for you to bring to life during your year in Paris. Your special thoughts, your precious experiences can be relived in future years. Bon voyage. We will miss you and love you always." On the first page I write that this book belongs to me not because my name is embossed on the cover but because of my father's inscription inside.

That year in Paris the city explodes, and I spend much of it behind student barricades and dropping acid in the Bois de Boulogne. My writings are the scribblings of a tormented soul—angry diatribes, lonely pleas, a brief fling with a butcher's son who sang partisan songs as we crossed the Champ de Mars at four in the morning, and some generic rage at my parents for being part of the problem and not the solution. Not much came of my early scrawls and rants and poetic outpourings. Yet I was drawn to the word, cliché though it is, as the moth to the flame. After that year abroad I always kept journals, never thinking that they'd ever see the light of day. Or that I would have the nerve to call myself a writer. Still I wonder if my father knew that he was sending me off on an even greater journey than the one I embarked upon to France.

15

India, 2011

IT IS SO COLD in Pench that the bananas have frozen on their stems. The crimson hibiscus that grows around the hotel and the tomatoes in the vegetable patch have all turned brown. Still, there is a warm sun beating down as we pull into the Pench Jungle Camp. The hotel is made up mainly of tents with some bungalows. I am in tent #2, and I'm amazed at how toasty warm it is, and spacious, with a nice bathroom. I've never really stayed in a tent before, so I like the rustic feel. I quickly settle in and, though I am tired, I head out immediately for a walk on the grounds. There are flowers everywhere and the air is filled with butterflies. Tiny blues, huge white ones, lots of black swallowtails with red speckles on the end of their wings.

Dinesh leaves me soon after we arrive. He is staying in town. I don't know where and I have no way of reaching him, but he assures me that he will return in five days. For hours, as we drove down, he talked nonstop. It was a little like sitting next to an insane person on an airplane. All I could do was listen. Still, after he leaves, I realize that I am startlingly alone. Not just without someone to talk to, or rather to listen to, but I fear, correctly it seems, that I am the only guest at the hotel. It is midweek and winter and no one else is here.

That afternoon I find a place to rest in the garden in the sun. It is near a fire pit filled with ash. Around the pit is a circle of chairs and I collapse into one. The warm sun beats on my face, and I soak it in, but soon the air starts to cool and by four I go inside. I struggle not to fall asleep reading and decide to have dinner as early as I can.

The darker it gets outside, the colder the air. It's just a little after six when the sun goes down, and I head to the dining room. Clearly this is the off-season. The room is empty except for the servers. Dinner is a buffet of creamy chicken curry, lentils, and rice. A waiter with a pitcher of water stands just to the side of my table, watching me eat. It is rather disconcerting. It is also freezing in the dining room, which has nothing but screens and more or less open doors. I am so cold it surprises me. And now there's no way around it, I am getting sick. Really sick. Not the kind of sick you get in India. I've been around the world too many times, I think, for that. I am getting hit with a very bad virus, a kind I get only when I am run-down.

My throat is killing me. I am coughing and my head aches. I ask for tea. Lots of it. I'm still hoping this is exhaustion from the travels, but I remember that I was starting to feel sick even before I left home. I told it to go away and it did—until now, when it seems to be blossoming inside my chest. I try to convince myself that what I need is rest. It is still early as I head back to my tent, but I am tired and I have a jeep picking me up at six in the morning to take me on my first tiger safari. I think I will read, take a bath, maybe do some writing. As I follow the dark path back to my tent, I can see my breath. Later I will learn that this is one of the coldest winters in India in recorded time.

I am grateful for my cozy tent until I step inside. Now it is just as cold inside as outside. The warm air of the afternoon has leached away. The tent has no insulation. I am inside only a moment or two before I am shivering. I decide to take a shower because at least that will warm me up. The bathroom itself is completely exposed to the elements. I may as well be in the woods. I turn on the shower and wait, but it doesn't even get warm. I wait, fiddle with the valves, but no matter how long I stand there, my teeth chattering, there's nothing I can do. Not only do I not have heat or protection from the cold, I have no hot water either. Perhaps there is hot water only during the day.

I don't want to complain. I rinse off as best I can and decide a shower will have to wait until tomorrow. I have my hot-water bottle with me, thanks to Susan, and I scurry back to the main house, where a group of hotel workers are sitting in winter coats, watching a Bollywood film. One of the men notices me and takes my hot-water bottle—no questions asked (the problem is obvious). For a few moments I sit trembling in the main hall, the Bollywood film in black-and-white piercing the night in what I assume is Hindi. When the man brings the bottle back to me nice and hot, I race to my room, clouds of breath in front of my face. I thrust the hot-water bottle under the covers. A few moments later I slip into the sheets. My hands are too stiff from the cold for me to write. I'm too cold to read. And my throat is on fire.

In my layers of clothing I wrap myself around the hot-water bottle. I sip from the flask of whiskey Dinesh bought me—more perhaps to calm my nerves than to soothe my throat. I drift off this way, but when I wake in the middle of the night, the hot-water bottle has grown cold and for the rest of the night I lie trembling in my tent. I hate to be cold. I think it must be because of my Mediterranean blood. I'd much rather lie around like an old sloth in the heat than shiver like this in bed. I lie there, barely sleeping, wondering what the point is. What am I trying to prove by traveling all this way—halfway around the world—alone? Perhaps the time has passed for me to engage in such escapades. I've lost my edge. I should stay closer to home.

16

IN FOREST PARK, QUEENS, in 2004, a 450-pound Bengal tiger named Apollo walks out of his cage that is inadvertently left open in a circus trailer. He strolls past sunbathers, a choir group, and families hosting barbecues, and then he climbs onto the Jackie Robinson Parkway. Unsure of what to do, he pauses as drivers, in disbelief, crash into one another. Some abandon their cars, dashing away. One couple shrieks as the tiger jumps on their hood. No one is hurt. Shortly thereafter his trainer lures him back. Apollo, who has known only his cage, goes willingly.

17

New York, 2010

ON A BRIGHT December morning just weeks before I am to leave, I'm up early. I have to go get my visa to India. It's a freezing-cold morning and I bundle up. I have a reservation and, surprisingly for me, I arrive on time, only to find a line out the door. I thought the fact that I had a 10:40 a.m. reservation would be relevant, but apparently it is not. The guy before me had a 9:40 a.m. reservation. It's going to be a long morning and I have to get to work. It is the last few days of the semester.

I'm perhaps fifteenth in line so I think I should go and tell the Hispanic guard with the walkie-talkie and the wire in his ear that I have an appointment. I'm not certain that everyone ahead of me does. A woman in a fur coat with a red-dyed fur hat is putting on her mascara behind me and I ask her if she'll hold my place. "I'm not in line," she tells me in a thick Russian accent.

As I approach the guard, a Russian man (the husband of the woman in fur, it turns out) with a lot of dandruff is shouting about not having an appointment but needing a visa. He's going into a long, complicated story about his documents and why his passport has expired and his need to travel, but the guard will have none of it. "Go to the back of the line, sir."

Just then an elderly Indian man approaches and says that he too has to get a visa and he can't wait. "Do you have a reservation, sir?" the guard asks. The man replies he does not but he requires a visa. "But do you have a reservation?" Once more the man says he does not. This elderly gentleman who is nicely dressed with a cap on his head begins shouting at the security guard.

The Russian is still trying to explain his problem, but

the guard starts shouting back at the Indian gentleman that he needs a reservation. Around me a Sikh in an orange turban yells into his cell phone in a language I don't recognize. Other people of Indian descent are also on their phones, some crying, some begging for documents from family members. "I need my birth certificate," one girl sobs. "Fax it to me."

The elderly gentleman refuses to take no for an answer, and the guard calls for backup. "I need help down here," he says. A woman appears in some official capacity, and the guard shouts at her in Spanish, "I need someone to tell this asshole to go away." I'm not sure who else in this line understands him, but I do.

Finally the manager of the visa office, who looks and acts a bit like a former marine, comes outside in his shirtsleeves on a freezing day. "No walk-ins, absolutely no walk-ins. You must have a reservation," he shouts in a distinctly German accent to the angry elderly gentleman and the Russian man, who are now both screaming. There's lots of rumbling from the crowd. Some people leave. Many do not have a reservation. The line shortens. I am making progress. After about half an hour, I am first in line. I am told to turn off my cell phone and prepare my documents, which I do. I feel the tinge of excitement. Soon I will have my visa.

But upstairs there are two more long lines, one that snakes around, and one where you have to wait to get your documents examined. After about fifteen minutes a woman asks me to come up to the front. She looks over everything. "All is in order," she tells me—except I don't have enough pages in my passport for the India visa and therefore I am denied.

"What do you mean?"

"You need visa pages in your passport. You have only one page available. You need two."

"But nowhere does it say I need two." I am displaying the sheet of instructions for the India visa that I got off the Internet.

"Well, you do."

This is what I get for traveling so much.

I am told I have to go to the U.S. passport office and there I will be issued new pages or a new passport, depending on what I prefer, but that I have to make an appointment for this and that can take several days (which it does). Before leaving I think I should make another appointment for my visa, but on the way to the computers, I run into the manager, who asks me my problem. I am aware of the fact that I am one of the few white people in the room and he hasn't asked anyone else what their problem is. I make a mental note of this as I explain about my passport pages.

He nods, makes a sweeping gesture at the room, which is filled with the troubled, turmoiled masses, snaking slowly around in their lines. "Why don't you just mail your application in?"

"Can I?"

"Why would you ever want to come back here again?"

The question for him is clearly rhetorical, and I can't help but note the disdain in his voice. His message to me is coded. Because it is clear to him that I am white and educated and many who frequent his establishment are not. I decide then that I will not mail my application; I will return in person if I can.

As I walk out, the Hispanic bouncer asks me why I'm leaving so soon. "My passport doesn't have enough pages."

He shakes his head, his voice filled with pity. "That's a bummer," he says.

On the packed subway, heading to Grand Central, I need to write some of this down, but I have nothing to write on. So I take out a piece of paper and try to scribble notes on the pole. A young man asks if I want to sit down. "No, thank you. I'm getting off at the next stop."

"But you're trying to write on that pole." I shrug and he holds up his hand to me. Not knowing what else to do, I high-five him. He looks a little stunned, then bursts out laughing. "I was holding it up for you to write on it," he says.

As we pull into Grand Central, I wish him a good day. On the train to work I nibble from the snack bag Larry prepared for me. My purse is always filled with all kinds of things—gloves, water bottles, snacks, pens, Life Savers. I'm not paying that much attention. I'm reading and nibbling. Then I eat a dog treat. Apparently I also have a bag of these.

I sit back, gazing as the train crosses the Harlem River,

a part of my commute to work I always love. It's a gray day and the river reflects the pewter sky.

My new passport arrives with its pristine pages via FedEx and, as soon as it does, I make an appointment online and march back to Travisa for my visa. The lines are, of course, long, but everything is at last in order. Behind me a young couple is heading home to celebrate their engagement. An old woman stands in line with tears in her eyes. Tired masses, huddling, pushing, wanting to get the sticker in their passport that will allow them to cross half the world and go to India. College students about to travel, a businessman with an air of self-importance stands in front me, tapping his papers against the palm of his hand. Perhaps he should have mailed in his work the way the manager had urged me to do.

I have my paperwork in hand. In the space marked "Profession" I have written "Writer." Normally I would not be so bold. I have traveled all over the world and have always, as a precaution, listed my profession as "Teacher." In the former Soviet Union, in Cuba, in China, I also indicated that I am a teacher. It raises less eyebrows, causes no problems. But this time I don't want to. Somewhere Toni Morrison wrote that men have no problem calling themselves writers, but that women are less emboldened. So I feel brave. I am going off to write and wander on my own. This time, for this trip, I am proud of myself. I am a writer and that is what I put down on my visa application.

When I reach the front of the line, I turn in my paperwork. The woman looks it over. "All right," she tells me. "It looks like everything is here." She tells me to return the next day and pick up my visa. It is Wednesday and on Monday I leave for India, and my excitement is palpable. It is done. I am almost ready to leave. Now I can focus my attention on packing, on research, on going through my checklist. I am trying to ignore the fact that I feel a soreness in my throat. I cannot get sick, I tell myself. I am going to push this thought away. I start drinking hot liquids and swallowing tablets of vitamin C.

Thursday is a gray December day. Not cold really. Just a kind of gray nothing hangs over the city. It is the end of the month. In two days it will be New Year's Eve. The day after New Year's Kate will move with her boyfriend to D.C. and the day after that I will fly to India. It is all what it is going to be. More or less set in stone.

I return to see many of the same people who were in line with me the day before. The young couple in love, the old woman, the impatient businessman. And I watch as each of their names is called and they disappear out the door, smiles on their faces, travel documents in hand. Their adventure is about to begin. I wait, but my name isn't called. Still, there are others who haven't received them. I tell myself not to panic. Maybe it's like when you're waiting for your luggage and it's going to be the last bag off the plane. But it is taking a long time. As I sit, I realize I am feeling weak. Almost faint. I have a bottle of juice with me and I sip it. There is a slight stinging I decide to ignore at the back of my throat.

Before long only a few of us remain. This is about when you'd start to fill in the "lost luggage" forms. I take a seat on a plastic chair next to a young man who appears to have been waiting for a while as well. He's doing the *Times* crossword puzzle and it's a Thursday, so I am impressed. I decide to make conversation. Perhaps he knows something that I don't know. "Have you been waiting long?"

He nods. "I had to get some things straightened out."

"Like what?"

"Well, I'm a photographer and they sent my passport to the media department . . ." He sees the look on my face. "What profession did you write down?"

I gulp. "Writer."

He shakes his head. "That might be a problem." Then he tells me that he had to wait three weeks for his visa, but he was on assignment for a magazine, so it didn't matter. "When do you leave?"

I am about to cry. "Monday."

His face fills with concern. "You better talk to someone."

It turns out the young man is correct. My passport and visa request have been sent to the media department of the Indian consulate and the problem is no longer being handled by the Travisa people. "But I'm not traveling on assignment," I tell the manager, who informs me that there's nothing he can do. It will take three to four weeks to process my request. "Oh my god, no." Tears swell in my eyes. "What can I do?"

The manager shrugs. "You need to discuss this with consular services."

I go back to the young man. "You're right," I tell him. "I should have written that I was a college professor." Oh, why didn't I do this? Why did I let pride get in my way?

"If you work for a college, get someone to write you a letter. The dean of your college or someone who can say that you aren't a writer but a professor of writing. Then go to the consulate tomorrow, not here." He gives me an encouraging smile, which I know he doesn't mean. "And good luck."

"Okay, okay," I tell him, thanking him profusely. I have no idea what I'm going to do, but it seems as if everything around me is falling apart. Did I really want to go to India? Do I really want to look for tigers? For the first time in my life I took travel insurance. I can cancel right now if I want. I call my husband in tears. Then I call Catherine, who is already in India. I explain to her that I may not actually be anywhere because of my visa problems.

"Listen," Catherine tells me, "I know all about these consular services. Bring a fruitcake."

"A fruitcake?"

"Yes, they love fruitcake."

I race home to write a letter to my dean. I draft the letter for him. "This is to state that Mary Morris is a tenured professor of creative writing" but that she's really not a writer at all. Or words to that effect. The dean faxes me a signed copy of the letter. Then I go to the store and buy a fruitcake.

18

WHY TIGERS? WHY ME? I have asked myself this question over and over. As I planned this trip that would take me into the heart of Asia. As I waited for my visa in New York. On the flight to Delhi. As I traveled south, I kept asking myself, Why have I come to the center of Madhya Pradesh? Is it just to search for one of the most elusive predators on earth? Or is it something more that draws me here? I think of Jorge Luis Borges and what he writes in his poem "The Other Tiger": "In South America I dream of you, / Track you, O tiger of the Ganges' banks." But for Borges the tiger remained in his dreams.

19

New York, 2010

ON FRIDAY, which is also the last day of 2010, I wake with a very sore throat. "I am not getting sick," I say over and over like a mantra, hoping that my body will believe it as I race out the door and join a seemingly endless line in the damp cold of December in front of the Indian consulate as people await their passports. Everyone has a similar problem. For one reason or another their visa has been denied or they need other official papers. Some need to file marriage papers and one man in front of me, I overhear, needs to ship his father's corpse.

It turns out that no bags are allowed inside the consulate and also there is nowhere to check them. However, a solution has been found for this dilemma. An enterprising young man has set up a private concession across the street. And literally on the street. For ten dollars each he will "check" your bags. That is, he will watch your briefcase, your backpack, anything bigger than a purse, as it sits on the sidewalk. Never mind that it is drizzling. That is where all the bags, including my backpack, end up. Unless, of course, you're one of the poor suckers (the grandmother in her sari, the impoverished-looking young man with his duffel) who don't happen to have ten dollars on them or an ATM card. They depart, dazed.

I relinquish my backpack, hold on to my papers, including the fax from the dean and a letter of my own explaining my status as a writer and that how this is all a huge mistake, and my fruitcake. Slowly the line seeps into the building, where we are squeezed into a small room that resembles the kind of institutional rooms where I imagine family members wait when visiting a prison. I am given some kind of a ticket with a letter of the alphabet. Clearly there are all kinds of problems being resolved, or just delayed, in consular services. Each clerk sits behind bulletproof glass. I put my fruitcake on the floor, wondering how I can slip it through the slot.

I'm starting to understand why Buddhism took root in India. Because Buddhism teaches you how to sit quietly and be present. And here everyone is sitting with seemingly endless patience. But I'm not like them. I am more like one of the Three Senseless Creatures: the monkey for its greed, the deer for its lovesickness, and the tiger for its wrath. And now my inner tiger is growing as I wait for my name to be called and my passport returned.

I do have a mantra. I got it in the Summer of Love and use it to this day. It's perhaps the one thing that I've never shared with a soul. Now I'm trying to use it as the minutes tick away. But it's hopeless. Instead I'm biting my cuticles and sighing deep, exasperated sighs. Doubts run through my mind. Maybe this is a sign. Maybe I don't really want to go on this trip after all. Maybe I shouldn't go—no matter what. I am contemplating this as, at last, my ticket is called.

I race up to the window and show them the fax from the dean, my own letter, a copy of my ticket for Monday. The woman looks it over. I am wondering if it is too late to retrieve my fruitcake and thrust it at her. Her expressionless face scans my materials. "Come back on Monday," she tells me. "We are closing early today for the New Year."

On Monday? "My flight is on Monday," I tell her, fighting back tears.

"Come early," she says.

I try to argue with her, but it is useless. I slip out, leaving the fruitcake on the floor behind me. I claim my checked bag from the sidewalk where rain has drizzled on it and make my way home.

The weekend is a haze. I pack, but only halfheartedly. Probably I'm not going anywhere. Instead, I help my daughter as her boyfriend prepares to move her and our dog to D.C. It's a dreary New Year's Eve. We have parties to go to, but I have the heart for none. Her boyfriend has driven up with a U-Haul van, and we help as they load the bins of clothing, her desk, her bike, two boxes of books, and the dog she's come to claim as her own. My child, who of course is now a grown woman, is going off into the world. I wish I could be like the grizzly bear who, when the time comes, chases away her cub. But that is not who I am. It is as if she is being wrenched from my arms, and I know that I must let go. When they leave, I rummage around the empty house. I rinse some dishes. I go to her room and start to sweep and clean up. It's pretty messy, so I get the vacuum, the Mr. Clean. I scrub and sweep, but in the end it's just an empty room.

On Monday morning Larry heads for work and I return to the consulate. We say goodbye, knowing that we will see each other either in a month or that night for dinner. I really have no idea which it will be. By ten a.m. I am at the consulate—this time with no backpack, no bribes. Just me, cup in hand. The wait is short and I go in right away. Apparently most of the people here last week were heading home for the holidays.

I sit on a plastic chair, staring at the floor. In four hours I might leave for the airport or be making a shrimp stir-fry. Half an hour later a woman emerges from behind the bulletproof glass. She hands me my passport, visa in place. It is so anticlimactic I hardly know what to say. I gaze at the visa and see that, despite the requirement of two blank pages, the visa has taken up only one. "Have a good trip," the woman bids me, and I'm out the door.

20

THERE ARE NO FLOCKS, no herds, no swarms or prides of tigers. Unlike lions, there is no word for tigers together. That is because they never are. The tiger's solitude is legend. There is no pack, no murder as with crows, no social structure. Except for a voracious twenty-four hours of mating, the male will seek no companionship. He will have nothing to do with the female or his cubs, though she will often share her kill with him. Perhaps to stave him off from eating his young. And the female, except when she is raising her cubs, is on her own.

It is a friendless life. Unlike crows, who have wild parties and often visit their parents even years after they have flown the nest, the tiger, once grown, except when mating, is always alone.

21

THERE WAS A TIME when I drank too much and smoked whatever I could get my hands on. I also went through a series of one-night stands. Once on a bus, a woman gets on, dressed as a baby. She wears a baby's dress, a diaper, and she's sucking on a bottle. She's an old woman so the contrast is particularly startling. I start to laugh and so does the man sitting across from me. He's blond, handsome, about my age.

When we get off at the same stop, we chat, and when we reach our mutual corners, we laugh. "Clearly we're going the same way," he says. He asks if I want to come up for a drink. I go to his apartment—a bachelor pad on West Seventy-Fifth Street near mine—and we start to drink and smoke weed and then we begin to make out. Suddenly I pull away. "Are you going to kill me?" I say.

22

PEOPLE THINK that being a writer is a lonely job, but I am rarely lonely when I'm writing. It is only in the morning when I first wake up and once the sun goes down that my demons revive. My demons. Where do they come from? Why are they here? That is a long story, perhaps another story, one I don't fully understand, but it is as if every morning I must battle them back into the cave from which they emerge. When I was younger, it didn't seem possible that a woman could be a writer and have a "normal" life— whatever that is. My model was my mother, after all, who should have had her own fashion line and instead taught my Brownie troop how to candle eggs. I imagined a life for myself not so different from hers—teaching, raising a couple of kids. Perhaps a suburban life. A country club. A life I cannot fathom now.

For years before I marry and have a child my routine is the same. Write all day. Go out at night. During the day it is solitude I seek. I need to settle into my own thoughts or they will never come. I can't work if someone is cleaning my house or fixing a faucet. It isn't quiet I seek but silence. And not just silence but the profound silence that comes from being alone inside of your head.

Recently I realized that silent is an anagram for listen. It is the voice that comes from the silence that the writer or artist must listen to.

23

India, 2011

AT SIX IN THE MORNING there's a knock at my door. A man stands there with a tray of tea and biscuits. As I thank him, once more I can see my own breath. I hand him my hot-water bottle and ask if he could fill it for the morning safari. He nods as if he understands, and I scurry back inside, ready for a shower but the water is still ice-cold. I leave it on and wait but still nothing. Finally I take a cold rinse off, throw on a pair of jeans. I put on all the layers I have—a long-sleeve T-shirt, sweatshirt, and fleece vest, much of which I'll peel off in the heat of the day, and head out to the open-air jeep that, apparently, tigers don't jump inside. Or at least thus far they have not, though I can't see what is to stop one.

My driver, Sudhir, is waiting for me. With his handle-bar mustache, khaki fatigues, safari hat, and vest he looks as if he walked out of *The Jungle Book*. As I fling myself into the jeep, scratchy horsehair blankets are tossed over my legs. Then someone runs back into the inn and returns with my hot-water bottle, which is piping hot. I slip it onto my lap. I am coughing, hacking, sneezing, and trying to control it. And I am swallowing, one after the other, the Halls cherry cough drops that Dinesh bought for me on the road.

It can't be much above freezing as we head out into the darkness before dawn. In the distance there is the first hint of sun, a sliver of light in the sky, but it is not enough to warm the air. We bounce on the furrowed dirt road for about half an hour until we come to what seems to be a small village, and there ahead of us in the predawn light I can see the gate that is the entrance to Pench. Near the gate dozens of men in green uniforms sit in folding chairs. These are the mandatory guides. Every jeep going into the reserve must have a driver and a professional guide. Here Sudhir pulls over. He bounces out of the jeep and tells me to wait. I nod, huddled beneath the horsehair blankets, gazing into the morning mist.

To my left in the field stand tall platforms upon which men sleep on straw pallets. Some of the men are waking, stretching. Beneath them the small fires that warm them at night are now no more than embers, sending smoke into the air. These men are hired to guard the fields and keep the wild animals away. A long rope extends from their platform into the fields. If an animal comes through their area, the rope will pull and the man somehow is supposed to chase the creature away. Now, as we wait for our guide, it is a strange sight to see these half-naked men, warming their hands at the waning fires.

For almost an hour we are motionless. I keep a scarf wrapped around my throat and the hot-water bottle, which is growing tepid by the minute, in my lap, but I can't seem to stop coughing. I'm popping cough drops and I'm going to be running out soon. From the thermos at my feet I sip warm tea—nervous not to sip too much because I'm not sure where the first pit stop will be.

The sun rises and a thin line of scarlet appears in the east, but everyone is freezing. The men on the platform, the guides, children riding their bikes to school, everyone is chastened by this chill. It's almost seven-thirty when a bespectacled young man jumps into our jeep. He has a woman's bright pink wool scarf wrapped around his head, and Sudhir seems very happy to see him, but the man barely nods at me.

24

THERE ARE MANY FORMS of camouflage in nature. The stick insect, the squid's ink, the tiger's stripes. Her stripes have evolved so that she can blend in with the grasses in which she crouches during the hunt. The tiger is speedy for only a short distance. She is built to pounce, not to race or climb. She can rarely outrun her prey, so she depends upon the element of surprise. If the tiger cannot hide, she will starve. The tiger is a very patient animal. She knows how to wait. She knows how to allow her stripes to blend in with the reeds and grasses that surround her. What she lacks in speed, she makes up for in stealth. Still, she is successful only about 30 percent of the time.

25

I START MANY THINGS that I never complete. My studio is littered with scraps of paper, tidbits, articles torn from newspapers and magazines. A note about a man driving with his family, who takes a wrong turn in the snow. A list of the warning codes aboard cruise ships. Random titles without stories. Pages without direction. A genealogy chart for the characters in a novel that has stalled. On the floor are piles of drafts for novels and screenplays. About a third of these will ever see the light of day. The rest will linger and eventually fade. Still, I can't help scribbling down any idea that comes my way. A flash of something that otherwise might elude me. I write to remember.

"Hold on to your hunger," my friend, David Lehman, once wrote. "It's your greatest asset."

26

THE PAINTER Joan Mitchell was once married to my cousin Barney Rosset (the famed publisher of Grove Press and the black sheep of my family). Barney and Joan grew up together in Chicago, and she was perhaps the love of his life. Something I read in a biography about Joan has stayed with me. When she was a sad little girl, Joan used to pull back the yellow curtains in her family's living room and stare at Lake Michigan. The lake brought her solace from a lonely and perhaps abusive childhood. Years later, many of her canvases contained blue and yellow. All of her paintings, it is said, began with the curtains and the lake.

I also grow up on the shores of Lake Michigan and we also have yellow curtains. My mother has an innate love of blue and yellow. Recently I learned that those are the most soothing colors to go together. To me it was always an interesting combination and a testament to my mother's artistic nature. She has a degree in fashion from the Art Institute of Chicago, and she's a gifted seamstress and artist. She used to paint in our basement, and I recall one portrait. A woman who looked much like herself except that half of her face is black. And the other half blue. I have often wondered if this wasn't her self-portrait. The first time I see it I don't ask because I'm too young, and when I'm old enough, my mother says she does not remember the painting.

We can't see the lake from our house. Not really. If I go to my parents' bedroom window, I can see a sliver of it. But we live only three doors down from the lake and if you just step outside, you smell the water. And sometimes in the late summer the dead fish. One summer all the alewives die and almost no one goes out, the stench is too great and the flies are too prolific. But I go to the lake every day. Even when I'm very young, my mother isn't afraid to let me roam. Despite not having much happiness inside its walls, outside of our home I'm a fairly happy child and free-ranging is what I love most. I comb the bluffs and follow the old Indian trails. I search for arrowheads, bear (which are long gone by the time we live there), and various other objects that my imagination finds a place for in suburban Illinois.

Mostly I roam to get away from my mother. She and I have a fractious relationship even when I am small. Once when I'm no more than ten, I need new clothes and my mother gives me sixty dollars, which is a lot of money in those days. She tells me to go to Fell Company and buy some new outfits for myself. I remember riding on my bike, dashing into the store, trying on outfit after outfit. All for summer and spring. I buy three or four that I like and pedal home. My mother immediately asks me to try them on, which I do. She doesn't like any of them and she takes them all back. One I like a lot is a lemon-yellow shirt with matching Bermuda shorts.

As I stand in front of her, my mother shakes her head. "Yellow is not your color," she says. To this day I have never worn yellow.

27

A HARVARD UNIVERSITY study shows that creative people tend to remember their childhoods as unhappy even if they were not.

28

India, 2011

WE GOT ONE OF THE BEST guides in all of India," Sudhir tells me, proudly pointing to the silent, bespectacled young man who has plunked himself in our jeep. Sudhir turns to me and beams. Clearly this is an honor to him, and I thought it must also mean a piece of good luck for me. But Ajay hasn't said a word since he leaped into our jeep. And he looks a little odd with the bright pink woman's wool scarf wrapped around his head, but Sudhir seems happy to see him. Ajay barely nods at me.

I am eager, waiting for the lecture that doesn't come. I'm not sure what I expected, but I assumed Ajay would start to explain something about the tigers or what we were going to see. That is, I thought I would learn something from him, as one does from a guide, but he doesn't even tell me his name. Sudhir does. In fact, Ajay says nothing to me at all. He sits up front in the passenger seat, staring ahead. It can't be much above freezing, and we've already been sitting here for more than an hour. I'm hugging my hot-water bottle that grows tepid by the minute and sucking on cough drops, trying not to let them know how sick I am.

Now the sun has risen, and we're waiting for the tiger reserve to open. Despite the cold and my illness, I am filled with anticipation. A blaze of scarlet cuts across the sky, but everyone is freezing. The morning in Pench has begun. It is almost eight. When I think I can't sit here any longer, the gates open, and we are motioned to move ahead. We bounce on the furrowed dirt road for about half an hour until we come to what seems to be a small village, and there ahead of us I can see the gate that marks the entrance to Pench.

The gate to the game reserve is open, and ours is the second of the dozen or so jeeps waiting to go in. As we enter on the dusty road, the jungle is lush, but oddly still. I thought I'd be seeing wild animals swinging on the vines, but the trees and branches are empty. Ajay and Sudhir mutter to each other. It seems that I am not the only one affected by the cold. The animals don't like it either. They have remained in the warmth of their caves or dens or the groves where they huddle. We drive for more than an hour and hardly see a thing. A few langur monkeys shake the branches of the trees. A baby langur squawks on the ground in distress until its mother scoops it up. Ajay and Sudhir laugh, but Ajay says little.

He is a bit of a conundrum, really. I am starting to wonder if he isn't just along for the ride. And I have the impression that he doesn't speak any English. Not that he must, but it would be easier for me to communicate with him if he did. And again I am confused about his role as my guide. How is he guiding me exactly? For a long time we're bouncing up and down the potholed roads. They chat between themselves in Hindi. Even if I lean in from the backseat, they make no attempt to talk to me.

I sit back and decide to wait, when suddenly Ajay raises his hand and Sudhir pulls to a halt. No one says a thing. We sit for ten or fifteen minutes. "Excuse me, but—" I start to ask what we are waiting for, but Ajay shushes me. He cups his ear to indicate that he is listening. I don't know what he's listening for because I hear nothing except for the call of some birds, the shriek of a monkey. Still, it is peaceful sitting in the quiet of the jungle. It is a kind of quiet I don't think I've ever heard before (if one can hear quiet, that is). Every rustling of the wind, every flutter of wings, is as clear and clean as pure water.

Then Ajay points in a direction. Sudhir starts the engine, the quiet is gone, and we go that way for a few moments. We stop again and listen. "We are listening for alarm calls," Sudhir explains in a hushed tone, and even that seems to annoy Ajay, who flashes a grimace his way. The alarm call is the sound an animal makes when the tiger is near. There is a sound for the mother calling her young; another to bring the herd together. And the animals make a different sound if the tiger is near. That is what Ajay is listening for. I'm trying to listen as well but I hear almost nothing. A high-pitched cry now and then that seems far in the distance.

I am more perplexed than bored. I am, after all, in a jungle in India and somewhere out there tigers lurk. But Ajay has explained nothing of his method of tiger tracking. He is pointing to the left, hand to his ear, when I catch a flash of emerald green out of the corner of my right eye. "What was that?" I ask, not really expecting an answer. Besides, Ajay is looking in the opposite direction.

"Green bee-eater," he replies without turning around. These are his first words to me.

I'm stunned. The bird was behind him. "How do you know?" I ask. "You didn't see it."

"By the sound of the wings," he replies.

And then we fall silent again.

29

A STUDY shows that if an American schizophrenic hears voices, they tell him to commit violence. And if a schizophrenic in India hears voices, they tell him to clean the house.

30

Brooklyn, 2008

THERE'S A BLIZZARD THAT DAY. At least that's what I'm told. And that's what it looks like as people clomp in and out of the emergency room, covered in snow. But I don't know what the weather is doing. I don't even care. I barely understand what is happening. I know I'm going to have what's called "reduction." To me a reduction is something you do to a sauce. You boil it down. But an ankle? At last I am put under, during which time my ankle is popped back into place. I assume that that will be that. But hours later I'm still in the emergency room on a morphine drip.

I remember being cold. Shivering. Doors open and close and frigid breezes filter in. I ask for blankets. It seems as if I keep asking. But the blankets aren't enough. The chill is in my bones. Larry rubs my hands and my arms, trying to get me warm. He can't bring himself to look at my foot. I drift in and out of what might pass for sleep, waiting for a doctor to tell me that this is somehow all a big mistake.

Just sign here and you can go home. On the wall in front of me is a clock and the hands keep going around the way they do in those old black-and-white films, as if time is flying by.

Toward evening a doctor appears. He is an anesthesiologist and he informs us that I'll be operated on that night. Operated? I don't understand. He tries to explain to me about the bone being in several pieces. How I will need a plate in my leg. "Can I go to Morocco?" I ask. I have plans for my sabbatical, and I think he almost laughs.

"We're going to put you in a room for now," he says, patting my hand. "And you should get some rest." But more hours go by before they wheel me into a room. In the next bed a comatose woman whimpers as Larry and I wait for a surgeon to show.

When the floor nurse comes in to check on me, we ask what time the surgeon will come. She looks at me with disdain. "No one is going to operate on you at this hour," she tells me in a flat voice.

"But they said in the ER . . ." I'm holding on to the thin thread of hope that the sooner they operate—even if it is only a matter of hours—the sooner I'll be on the mend. How long can this take? I'm viewing this as an unfortunate detour, a brief derailment. Like a flat tire or a wrong turn. A month or so max and I'll be on my feet.

"I don't care what they said, you won't have a surgery tonight." I search her face for a touch of compassion, a glimmer of hope, but there is none.

"Would you just call down to the OR and make sure?"

Larry asks, making his voice as respectful as he possibly can. Already we're becoming versed in the language of hospitals.

In her cold tone, her face still expressionless, she says she will. "When did you last eat?" the nurse asks me. The idea of food has meant nothing to me, but now suddenly it does. I tell her I haven't eaten all day. "Well, you should eat something." She tells me she has no idea when in the morning I'll have my surgery. If I'm going to eat, it's now or never, she implies.

It's after midnight on a cold, snowy night. The cafeteria is closed, as are most of the restaurants nearby. On the brink of despair I ask Larry to go home and bring some of the pasta we have left in the fridge. A nice spaghetti Bolognese I made the night before. "And smuggle in some red wine," I beg. It's true I'm on a morphine drip and I can't say I am proud of myself or am thinking clearly, but this is what I ask for.

When he returns with a warm container of spaghetti and a thermos of Bordeaux, I eat and sip some wine. It's almost a picnic, except for the morphine and the throbs of pain that course through my body. We're just finishing when the phone in my room rings. It's odd to get a call at one in the morning in a hospital room, especially if no one knows you are here, but Larry answers and I can tell by the look on his face that something is wrong. He keeps shaking his head. "Oh, no," he groans, "but she's just eaten." He pauses, and I can hear the loud voices on the phone. "The floor nurse told us no one would operate on her at this hour."

There is more noise, more grumbling. Then Larry gets off the phone. In the two decades I've been with my husband, I've never known him to lose his cool—except for once with my father, and that was also coming to my defense. With that one exception, I've never seen him raise his voice at anyone about anything, but he goes out the corridor and he yells at that nurse, "You could have made a phone call. One phone call. There's a surgeon waiting for her right now."

The nurse glares at him, stony-faced, but says nothing as he uses the phone at her station to try and procure an ambulance to transport me to another hospital. But there is that blizzard and not a single ambulance, not even the Hasidic volunteer ambulance, available to transport me into the city, which is where our primary-care physician (who Larry manages to get on the phone at that hour) suggests we go. Larry returns and tells me that we have to stay here, at least until morning.

A few minutes later the nurse comes in and tells Larry that he has to leave. "This is a women's floor," she says. She glances at the comatose woman in the bed beside me.

"Then call security," Larry replies. "I'm not leaving." And he sits down in a vinyl chair and watches me all night.

At four in the morning a swarthy young man in green scrubs walks in. In my bleariness I see him shake my husband's hand. I gaze at the strong grip as Dr. Patel introduces himself. Later Larry tells me that he has a good handshake and that he trusted him right away. It is one of the things my father once said about Larry. He has a good handshake. In fact, I am lucky that night. Dr. Patel happens to be a highly trained trauma surgeon. He is furious with the nursing staff for not checking with him and for allowing me to eat. He tells me that he'll operate first thing in the morning. Doing the math, I realize it's already morning, but Dr. Patel looks as if he's good for several more hours—which in fact he is. Later I will learn that he is a man who rarely sleeps.

Meanwhile I drift in and out. Periodically opening my eyes, I see Larry sitting in a chair, holding my hand. I don't think he ever closed his eyes. I don't remember going in for surgery, but I remember waking up in the recovery room. Larry is there waiting, and he's brought some books. My foot is neatly swathed—like a baby, I think. I'm wrapped in blankets and finally not cold. And I'm not in real pain so I pick up Paul Bowles's *The Spider's House*, which I've been reading in preparation for our trip to Morocco. I open to where I left off and am soon engrossed.

I don't notice when Dr. Patel walks in, and he looks stunned. "I've never seen a patient sitting up and reading after surgery," he tells me.

"It's a good book," I reply.

"It's not that," he says. "You must be a very strong person."

I shrug. I don't know. I don't think so. I just want to read my book. But perhaps I am stronger than I think. Is he hoping that this is so? I've always been a good student. I know how to work hard. So, if I'm a good patient, if I follow orders, I'll be all right. If I rest and do what he tells me, I'll get better fast. "Can I go to Morocco in six weeks?" "Let's see." Dr. Patel shakes his head, still amazed that I'm sitting up in the recovery room, reading a book. His voice sounds optimistic. "Let's see how it goes." He tells me then that my fibula was shattered in seven places and that, for now, a four-inch steel plate holds it together. It is only much later that he will tell me that I had the worst fracture of the fibula he'd ever seen. He's a trauma surgeon so obviously he's seen a lot. A racehorse, he'll tell me, is put down for less.

31

AT THE PALM BEACH ZOO in Florida a rare and nearly extinct Malaysian tiger mauls to death the female keeper, known as "the tiger whisperer," who took care of him. No one has explained what she was doing in the tiger's night enclosure. The zoo said that she was performing her normal tasks.

At the Amsterdam Royal Zoo a man scales a wall, crosses a moat, and enters a tiger's enclosure. Later, after the man dies, the Dutch police refer to this as suicide by tiger. And in the Bronx Zoo in New York a twenty-five-year-old man leaps from the monorail and scales a sixteen-foot fence, where a Siberian tiger named Bachuta more or less gnaws his foot off. The zookeepers in the Bronx were amazed that Bachuta didn't kill the man. The public was pleased that the tiger wasn't euthanized. "Bachuta did nothing wrong," his keeper said.

From his hospital bed the young man explained why he did this. "I wanted to be one with the tiger," he said.

32

India, 2011

THE WHITE TREE is known as the ghost tree. It does resemble a ghost. But among the drivers and guides it is also referred to as the Lady of the Jungle because she has big knots that resemble breasts. As Ajay and Sudhir manage to explain this to me by holding their hands in front of their chests, they are giggling like schoolboys. Then Ajay raises his finger, and we are silent. He turns to me in his halting English and asks, "Do you hear that?" I'm not sure what I hear. It sounds like a squeak that may be miles away. "That is sambar deer warning spotted deer. The tiger is near."

"The sambar deer warns the spotted deer?"

But Ajay doesn't have time to answer my question. Our

jeep is speeding off to the right along the rutted roads. I know that they have heard an alarm call. Peacock call, wild chicken call, spotted deer, sambar deer, barking deer, monkey, even the jackal and the wild boar, each has his rutting call, call to assemble, lost mother call, alarm call, and who knows what else. Ajay has learned how to listen to them all. He can hear the difference between a call to roost and a mother calling to her offspring, between a time to eat and a time to sleep, and the cry when danger is near. I cannot distinguish between any of the sounds he hears. What I am waiting for is the big roar, then the nine feet, four hundred pounds of tiger, four-inch claws extended, to come bounding out of the brush.

But Ajay can distinguish a bird by the flapping of its wings. The mother deer calling for her young. Amazed, I shake my head. It seems impossible but it's true. And he does speak some English, though he prefers silence in any language and I am fine with that. We push on and I try to listen for the alarm calls. I hear nothing, but Ajay says something to Sudhir and Sudhir turns to me. "Do you hear it? Sambar deer alarm call. Sambar deer warning white-tailed deer."

"You mean one kind of deer warns the other?" I ask again.

Now Ajay does his best to explain that the white-tailed deer makes an alarm call when it hears the tiger, but the sambar deer makes an alarm call only when it sees the tiger. "So if you hear the sambar call, then you know that the tiger is really there." I guess being able to tell the difference between the sambar and the white-tailed deer alarm calls must have something to do with his being the best guide in India. I nod, ready to learn more.

Ajay keeps his eyes to the ground. As he's looking for pugmarks—the footprints a tiger leaves—a ball of dust is coming our way. Another jeep filled with tourists approaches and halts next to ours. It looks like a single family. An older man and woman, two teenagers. As they peer out from beneath their horsehair blankets, not one of them smiles. They all have miserable, dour faces. Clearly, they haven't seen a tiger either. And their vacation is a bust.

Ajay and Sudhir and their guides speak rapidly in Hindi, asking, I assume, if a tiger is near. The guides are also grumbling. They work very hard at finding the tiger. "No tiger, no tips" is their saying. There seems to be a consensus and their jeep takes off in another direction. I am feeling lucky. I could easily be riding in a jeep filled with those grumpy people, but because my hotel is empty, I have Sudhir and Ajay to myself.

We sit in silence until I hear a distant, piercing shriek. "Is that it? Is that the alarm call?"

Ajay shakes his head. "Spotted deer calling for his mother." I'm still trying to understand how he hears such things. He is a sommelier of sound.

We come to a large, open field known as Alikatta where there are some outbuildings that look like offices and washrooms. Off to the side four elephants stand, chained. On a large flat grill men are making giant flat breads, or chapatis, the size of truck tires that the elephants will eat like crackers. A single elephant will eat twelve of these at a sitting. Or, well, a standing. With enormous wooden spoons the men are stirring the meal, adding water by hand, then flattening the mixture and laying it on the grill. These men are the mahouts who tend the elephants. Others—guards, guides, and some tourists—have come to warm themselves at the grill.

We are stooped, our hands near the flames, when suddenly the men at the small guard station start shouting. With their machine guns slung around their arms they are pointing. An alarm call has sounded. Ajay and Sudhir rush back to the jeep and I jump in behind them. We're off. We race in one direction, then another. We are skirting the area as the alarm calls are sounded. I, however, hear nothing. The high-pitched shrieks that the men hear are lost on me.

We pause. "You don't look for the tiger," Ajay tells me at one of our stops. "You will never find her. You look for signs of the tiger."

Then Ajay hears something, and we are off again.

33

AT TIMES I wonder why I need to see a real tiger in the wild. Why not just the tiger in my mind? The one I had once dreamed about. Certainly a zoo tiger won't do, but what's wrong with the one that I imagined so long ago? Pablo Picasso once told a friend that to him landscapes were foreign territories. "I never saw any. I've always lived inside myself. I have such interior landscapes that nature could never offer me ones as beautiful." If I imagine the tiger—her symmetrical stripes, her yellow eyes, the giant paws, the way she crouches and slinks through the jungle—isn't that enough? Why do I have to see the real thing when I can see her in my dreams?

Many years after Marc Chagall fled his beloved Vitebsk, he was invited back. He was an old man and much of the turmoil of the years that forced him to flee Russia were over. Chagall pondered the invitation but in the end he refused. He was worried that if he saw the real place, he would lose the one that he had been imagining for so long.

34

India, 2011

I GROW ACCUSTOMED to their rhythms. The silence, the stopping and listening, then starting up again. When Ajay is listening, his ears almost seem to perk up. If one of us speaks, he holds up his finger to silence us. He is like a concert master, listening for the viola that is out of tune. But still there is no tiger. "It is too cold for them," Sudhir says and Ajay agrees. Tigers like the heat. No one expected this cold.

Hours go by and we keep driving around. Every so often we run into the jeep, filled with that family of disgruntled tourists, wrapped in sweaters and blankets. Our guides stop and talk in Hindi. Where can the thirty-three tigers and twelve cubs that inhabit Pench be? But we are having good luck with woodpeckers.

We stay out even as the sun begins slipping below the trees, and no one has seen a tiger. The game park closes in an hour, and we begin to see our breath. Sudhir asks if I am ready to return to the hotel, but I want to stay out as late as we can. I am not ready to give up the search. Ajay and Sudhir seem pleased with my decision. We've come to a fork in the road and Ajay points to the right. "We will go a different way now," Sudhir says as we head off.

At closing time, as we leave the game park, we are silent but in a different way. I sense their disappointment. "We have a few more days," I say.

Sudhir and Ajay exchange looks, and Sudhir explains: "Ajay is our guide only for today. Tomorrow we will have another. They are taken in order." But I don't want another guide. I want the man who can hear the flapping of wings and know the name of the bird.

On our way we drop Ajay at his home in a nearby village. The road is dusty, and the houses are mostly made of mud. We pull up to a mud house. In front a young woman in a rose-colored sari is shaping dough. She is clearly with child. Ajay greets her, and then he goes inside. Given the odds of having the same guide tomorrow, I doubt that I will see him again.

35

I'M A RESTLESS CHILD. Flitting from place to place. My father nicknames me Pigeon because I never sit still. It is a name that sticks. (My mother just calls me "Mary, Mary, quite contrary." This is her explanation for my behavior. I am, I suppose, a stubborn, headstrong child.) But what I want, if I can now put a word to it, is freedom. Something I still crave. Something that can be elusive now.

I love butterflies, and at one point I have an extensive collection of them—fragile, beautiful creatures I capture with my net in the woods or later send for from a Latin American butterfly company. In high school I briefly contemplate a career as an entomologist. Flutterbyes, I call them as a child. And often just byebyes. I am not surprised when I learn that in Chinese the word for butterfly translates to "tiger ghost." In the jungle of Pench I watch them. Tiger ghosts floating by.

36

Brooklyn, 2008

"NON-WEIGHT-BEARING" is what Dr. Patel says. It's a term I hadn't heard before and will come to dread. He explains that I cannot put any weight on my foot until it is completely healed. At least two months and maybe three. And I can't go home from the hospital until I'm able to get around on one leg with a walker and go up and down stairs. An occupational therapist comes into my room to explain this to me and to show me the basic principles of the walker. Over the next two days I'll have a daily therapy session with her. "Then you can leave."

But I don't want to stay in the hospital for two more days. The few days I've been here, flat on my back, seem like more than enough. And the sooner I leave, I reason, the sooner I'll be on my feet again. Even one more day becomes unbearable to me—let alone to Larry, who has slept in a chair for the past three nights and has gone home only to shower and walk the dog. He is as exhausted as I am, but he refuses to leave me. Especially after the night when a nurse comes in, flicks on the lights, and gives me a pain injection. Then slips a bedpan under me and, without waiting for me to finish, walks out of the room. "I'm not leaving you," he insists. Still he is so tired. I see it in the sunken look in his eyes.

I'm anxious to return to my life and hungry for visitors,

messages. News from the outside world. I am desperate to get out of the hospital. The nurses are surly and at times downright mean. If Larry wasn't there, they'd ignore me for hours at a time. I can't eat the food and just being in the hospital makes me feel vulnerable. I'll never get well as long as I'm here.

An hour before my occupational therapy session, I ring for my pain medication. Even though I don't really need it yet, I want to be as numb as possible. I want to go smoothly through my drills and not reveal to the therapist the extent of my pain. The words of Dylan Thomas come into my mind: "Rage, rage against the dying of the light." I fear she won't let me go home. An orderly comes for me, and, when I get to the office, there is a small wait. A little bit of wheelchair gridlock. A man is in the room as well, waiting for his session. And two other people are in the treatment rooms, receiving instruction. I've hardly spoken to anyone in days and decide to make small talk. "So how long have you been here?" I ask.

The man is relatively young and good-looking, with sandy brown hair and pale blue eyes. He has a warm smile, even though he clearly moves with great difficulty and a good deal of pain. I'm assuming he's been laid up for at least a week or two. "Oh, I've been here on and off for the past three years." He gives a little chuckle.

I am stunned. And I'm complaining about a few days. "What do you mean?"

He was a truck driver and, while unloading cargo, his truck was struck by another vehicle, and he was pinned—

and virtually crushed—against a wall. He's been in physical therapy of some sort ever since. "They told me that after three years I probably won't get any better, so this is about it for me." His eyes well up.

Three years. Surely I'll be as good as new in three years. This will all be behind me, won't it? A depressing but fading memory. But it is a number I won't forget. Nor will I forget his sad eyes. I watch him, tears in my own eyes, until the therapist comes and puts me through my drills. I walk with the walker, moving it forward as I've been instructed, then hopping on one leg. I shimmy on my butt, up and down stairs. My therapist nods, obviously impressed. "Have you been practicing?" she jokes as she makes notes on her clipboard. She has no idea how desperate I am to get out of here.

I remember my uncle Herman in the last months of his life. In his nursing home he cruised the corridors, speeding in his wheelchair all night long. Nothing could make him rest. He's running away from death, one of the nurses said.

"You can go home," my therapist tells me as she signs my sheet. The doctor will sign off on it later. I give a wave to the man for whom every step is agony.

He purses his lips, nodding at me. "You'll be fine," he says.

Later that afternoon a peculiar young man shows up in my hospital room with an enormous wheelchair—big enough for two people. He stands by the side of my bed, babbling, staring up at the ceiling and pointing at the chair. I'm not sure who he is or what I am supposed to do. It seems as if there is some mistake. I'm not dressed yet. I haven't been told when I'm being discharged. "I need to get dressed," I tell the man, but he just stands there mumbling to himself. Larry, who is in my room, napping, wakes up. "I don't know what he wants," I say.

Suddenly the man turns around and runs away. Larry leaves to talk to the staff and see what is going on and, while he is gone, the young man returns. Behind him is a woman who is talking into a red cell phone. Putting her phone against her thigh, she explains. "You've been discharged. You're going home." The young man is mentally challenged and is here to wheel me out of the hospital. She also explains that it is his first day and I am his first patient.

"Does he know what to do?" I ask, somewhat dismayed.

"He's in training," the woman says. Then she has him bring the wheelchair over to the side of my bed, where, without either the woman or the young man bothering to help me, I swivel into it, keeping my leg raised.

As the woman continues her conversation on the phone, making her plans for the evening (should they meet at the restaurant or at her house?), the challenged young man speeds me through the narrow corridors, muttering under his breath, "Stay away from the walls. Stay away from the walls." He zips along as if this is a bumper-car race, and we have to win. I keep my eye on my leg as we careen toward the double automatic doors, which miraculously open and the young man stops at the taxi stand. Moments later Larry arrives, with my few belongings clutched in his hand, and guides me into a waiting cab.

Outside, it is cold. A damp chill in the air. I have been in the hermetically sealed walls of the hospital for days and the muted sunlight and cool air come as an awakening. I keep my face pressed to the window as we drive through the bleak February landscape of the neighborhood where I live. After a few moments the cab pulls up in front of our house, and as it drives away, I stand in the street, staring at the curb, unable to move.

The curb is no more than six inches high, but it is an insurmountable obstacle to me. Even with my walker I have no idea how I'm going to get over it. Larry sees me standing, shaking my head. "Steps," I remember my father saying angrily toward the end of his life as he tried to get into a doctor's office. "You didn't tell me there'd be steps."

Larry clasps his arms around me, lifting me up onto the sidewalk. From there I hop with the walker to our front stoop—the one I toppled down a week before—and slide up the steps on my backside the way the occupational therapist has taught me to do. And to think that a week ago I'd been worried about jury duty.

37

THE ROMANS used to crucify tigers to discourage others of their species from preying on humankind.

38

India, 2011

THAT EVENING I speak to the manager about how cold it is in my tent and that it doesn't really have hot water. He looks perplexed. "I'm a little sick," I tell him. I ask if perhaps I couldn't have an actual room. Given that I am the only guest, it isn't that hard for him to make an adjustment. There is a bungalow available. It is made of concrete, and he promises me it has hot water. Right after supper, where the waiter still stands beside me, water pitcher in hand, I move into the cottage, which is a bit more expensive, but at least it has walls and isn't open to the elements and the air. And I'm assured there is hot water. I'm a little embarrassed for making a fuss. My mother almost always changed hotel rooms and tables in restaurants.

My bungalow is tucked down a stone path at the edge of the woods. I like it right away. The worker who takes me there turns on the hot water to prove that it has hot water. He leaves the water running as he shows me the room—which in fact needs no explanation.

But we discover a large grasshopper sitting on my bed. It is bright green and the size of an ashtray. I am afraid he will kill it, but instead he gets a plastic cup from the bathroom, where the water is still running. Carefully the young man captures the grasshopper, and then cradles it in his hands. He steps out onto the patio to let it go, and the grasshopper hops away. Then the young man turns off the shower, content that I have hot water, and is gone.

I unpack, put my things into drawers, into the bathroom. I am thrilled to take my first hot shower since arriving in India. I turn it on and wait, but the water is ice-cold. I wait and wait, but there is still no hot water. The man was so anxious to prove to me that there was hot water, I reason, that he depleted my supply. I rinse off, deciding to postpone my shower until the next day. I lie down and immediately drift off. On the wall above my head is a painting. Shiva is playing a flute and the sacred cows are dancing.

39

New York, 2010

BEFORE I LEAVE on this journey, I see my internist, a lovely Chinese American woman who is conservative in her practices and very thorough. I go over some routine matters, some prescriptions that need refilling. Then I tell her that I am going to India and wonder what shots or pills I will need. "No problem," Dr. Kwok says blithely, opening a map of the world. She homes in on India. "Just where exactly are you going to be?"

I search around, pointing to the major cities, Delhi, Mumbai, Kolkata, to which she merely nods. To Varanasi, where she grows slightly more engaged, and then I put my finger on a large green patch in the center of India where Rudyard Kipling set his classic colonial story (though, oddly, he wrote it in Vermont) *The Jungle Book*. "And I'm going there." I'm pointing to the very core of the Indian subcontinent.

Dr. Kwok's eyes grow wide and for a moment she says nothing. Then, "You're going to need everything." Over a period of several weeks she inoculates me for all the infectious diseases she can except for the plague and Japanese encephalitis, which "shouldn't be a problem," as she puts it, unless I will be working in the fields near a contaminated water supply in summer. And she reminds me, as if I had to be reminded, that it is winter. I forget to ask for a prescription of antibiotics. Why would I need antibiotics?

40

MY MOTHER, standing on the stairs, is scolding me. Her red polished fingernail points in my direction. That is my first memory. But there are others that seem more confused. Am I really in a basket in the backseat as we drive to Indiana? A funnel cloud appears in the distance, touching down, and my father drives like a madman to beat the storm. And later me crying by a brook under a crab apple tree because my father had promised me a river and an orchard.

I recall the day when my brother was stricken with a mysterious illness. He's a newborn and it's summer, a bright hot summer day. I am three years old when my brother wakes up from a nap, gasping. He is only a few months old and his windpipe has closed. He has to be rushed to the hospital and my mother is taking him in a car. I don't remember who drove the car, but she is sitting in the backseat. A blazing summer day and I'm wearing shorts, a T-shirt. I'm standing outside with my nanny, who is dressed in white—a whiteness that is blinding. Everything else is green. The lawn, the trees. Though it is hot outside, in the car it is cool and dark. I know because I try to crawl in. My mother cradles my brother and just as they are about to leave, I jump into the car to hug her. Perhaps I fear she is leaving for good. Perhaps I only want to say goodbye, but she pushes me away. She shouts to the nanny, "Get her out of here."

My nanny, in the blinding whiteness, drags me away, crying, screaming.

A few days later we go to pick up my mother. I'm not sure if she's been home while my brother's been in the hospital, but I know we go to pick her up. My brother isn't with her. He has to stay in the hospital another day or so. But she is coming home. I'm in the backseat, staring out the rear window when I see her walking toward us. She's smiling in a snug gray dress, a hat, gloves. Her lipstick is bright red against the gray. It is a gloomy day, and all the leaves have fallen from the trees. Suddenly it is winter.

Years later, when I have grown up and moved away, it will occur to me that this cannot be. Only days before it was summer. But this is how I remember it.

41

WHEN THE NATIVE PEOPLE of Siberia hunt elk or deer, they always leave a haunch behind for the tiger. And in return the tiger always leaves something behind for them. For centuries they lived in harmony.

42

WHEN MY DAD turns eighty, I call to wish him a happy birthday, and he says, "I had the strangest dream last night." He isn't a person to talk about his inner life, but this is what he told me. He says that when he was four years old, his family moved to Nashville, and the night before they moved he had to sleep in a bed with his aunt and uncle. She was very fat and he was very skinny and

Dad couldn't breathe. "I haven't thought about that night in Nashville in seventy-five years, and now I remember it like it was yesterday." And then he starts to cry. "My whole life lives inside of me," my father says.

He lives another twenty-three years. When he is starting to fail, I have a dream. I dream that we are on a boat going somewhere. Just the two of us. On a river. We had once, when I was a girl, gone on an outing on the Fox River and I recall it as one of the few happy days of my childhood. That is, a day when he didn't lose his temper. In the dream it is evening and we are going to a party. Ahead on the river there's a house that is lit up with Japanese lanterns. People are milling about, having drinks, eating appetizers. There's a dock and my father drops me off. "Aren't you coming with me?" I ask him and he replies, "No, you'll be going back alone."

In May 2005 my father is dying. He is, after all, a hundred and three. He's so old that once when we tried to renew his heart medication, the pharmacist called to say that he can't fill this prescription for a three-year-old. We had to explain that his computer must have defaulted, and my father needs his medication. I have a ticket to go see him the day after my birthday. That evening Larry, Kate, and I go to *Show Boat* at Lincoln Center, a musical my father loved. I am eager to tell him about it. He used to sing "Ol' Man River" to me in his deep baritone, "*He don't say nothing, But must know something . . . He keeps on rolling along.*"

After the show as we're walking home, a woman in a heavy winter coat is barreling toward us, dragging a suitcase. I'm walking behind my family as she passes. When she comes to me, she raises her foot and kicks me in the gut, right into the street. For a moment I can't breathe. I'm shocked and in pain and Larry rushes me home. Shaken, I get right into bed, and a little later my brother calls. My father passed away half an hour before, almost precisely when the woman kicked me in the gut.

For months I'm lost. I go into a depression that I can't snap out of. My daughter is leaving for college and I'm going to go down the Mississippi River in a houseboat. I sink lower and lower. One night I have another dream. This one much darker. I am a schoolgirl in a uniform (something I never wore) and heading home. It's a bright sunny day. I pass a playing field where I see my father, umpiring at home plate. I call out but he doesn't seem to hear me. I call again and he turns. He looks right at me but he doesn't see me. He has no eyes.

43

WHEN YANN MARTEL was writing *Life of Pi*, the tiger was the third choice. First he tried the elephant, but it was too big for the boat. Then he tried a rhinoceros. Same problem. Then he came to the tiger.

44

Brooklyn, 2008

EVERY DAY that I'm laid up I cancel a hotel, a ferry ride, a flight. I call the keeper of a riad in the Sahara, I call the boat company that was to take us from Algeciras to Tangier. I tell them I've had an accident and won't be coming. Each stranger on the other end tells me that they are sorry. Some say they will pray for me. They all refund my money. I promise that I will come next year when I am well. Then I get off the phone and weep.

Other than these phone calls, I spend my days reading. There's not much I can do and little that I want to do. When I'm not canceling travel plans, dealing with my insurance, or fielding the calls of friends and neighbors asking how I am, I'm reading. In the fall I'll be teaching a class called the Writer and the Wanderer. I plan to focus on stories that happen during journeys, such as *A Passage to India* or *The Sheltering Sky*. *On the Road*. Then I decide to read *Death in Venice*. It is about a journey too, isn't it?

It is chilly in the den and I sit, my injured leg raised. I'm wrapped in a caramel-colored blanket I'd purchased that winter. That blanket is one of the few things that brings me comfort and eases my pain. I love snuggling into its soft, plush cotton. I want to be tired. I so want to be tired. But unless I'm taking medication or drinking wine, I'm wide awake. I just want the time to pass. I'm praying for sleep as I read the opening pages, but to the contrary I'm all wired up.

I read along for several pages until I come to a line that hits me like a bolt. As Aschenbach, the protagonist, decides he needs to get out of Munich, Thomas Mann writes, "He would go on a journey. Not far. Not all the way to the tigers." I stop, the book frozen in my hands. I can't read on. There are sentences that lie beyond this, but I can't bring myself to turn the page. I sit, mesmerized. I read this line over and over. It is as if no other words come after it. Tigers. The word ripples inside my brain.

Tigers.

Though I know little about them, they've always intrigued me. Mysterious beasts who travel alone. I am impressed by their solitude. I am drawn to their hunger. They've inhabited my dreams. What would it mean to go all the way to the tigers? What if I decide to do just that? Perhaps when my ankle is better, I will do this.

I put it on a mental bucket list. One more thing to do before I die. And then I forgot about it. It was an idea like so many others that at first seems incredibly important, essential at the time, then gets filed away. And is forgotten. For now I'm not going anywhere. For now I am staying home.

45

WENDELL BERRY WRITES, "It may be that when we no longer know what to do / we have come to our real work, / and that when we no longer know which way to go / we have come to our real journey." When I read this quote, it resonated with me. But now it resonates more. Perhaps for the first time in my life, I have no clear path. I have no idea what I'm going to do next. What seemed obvious just days before is now muddled and confused.

46

India, 2011

ONCE MORE at six in the morning there is the knock at my door. At least now I actually have a door and the bungalow is warmer than the tent. But still it is very cold as I tiptoe across the floor. Again a man stands there with a tray of tea and biscuits. I'm not very hungry, though the lemony tea feels good on my throat. I head to the jeep where Sudhir waits for me. My hot-water bottle is already tucked beneath the horsehair blankets. It is still dark out as I huddle under the blankets. We clomp along the bumpy road to the game preserve.

Again there is the wait as we pay the entrance fee and our papers are checked—a process that takes way too long.

Then we drive up to where the guides are waiting to be hired for the various jeeps. They must be taken in order. In the dim light I spot Ajay's pink scarf wrapped around his neck. He's sitting four or five seats down from the guide who is designated to be ours.

I tap Sudhir on the shoulder. "Isn't there anything we can do to have Ajay as my guide again?"

Sudhir looks at me and shrugs. "Well, you'd have to bribe the guy who is waiting first in line."

My heart sinks until Sudhir informs me that the bribe is the equivalent of two dollars. I hand Sudhir the rupees. The man is more than happy to agree. If he gets another jeep, he's made double for the day. And if he doesn't, he still comes home with a day's pay.

Ajay is the only person I want in the jeep. I have come to like his quiet, gentle way. I like the way he listens. I am amused by the pink wool scarf of his wife's that he wears against the cold and the way he chuckles when he pretends not to understand something that he does. Sudhir pays the bribe and waves. Once more the three of us are together. I feel less feverish, but I'm still coughing. They look at me, their faces filled with concern, but I pop a cough drop and look away.

When the gates open, we are among the first jeeps to enter because again we are one of only a few jeeps. From the trees above, langur monkey families stare down at us. We drive for a while until we are far away from the other jeeps, until the only sounds we can hear are those of the jungle. Then Sudhir pulls to the side of the road and turns off the engine.

For several moments we sit listening, watching. Ajay listens for the alarm calls of peacocks, monkeys, deer. I am in the back. I am always in the back. They are in the front, talking mostly in Hindi. I do not know what they are discussing but I assume it has to do with where the tigers might be. Or perhaps it is about me. About this sick, hacking woman who keeps insisting on going out in this startling cold on what might prove to be a futile mission. What we in the Old West call a wild-goose chase. But I like to think they are not talking about me. They are serious, thoughtful men. It is all about the tiger.

After a couple of hours we drive to the sunny spot in the middle of the preserve where the elephants are chained. The hotel has packed a snack of bread, cheese, and a piece of fruit, and we pause to eat it. On the fire, mahouts are frying up the chapatis for the elephants' lunch and the elephants, hungry and restless, tug at their chains. I use the bathroom and then we drive off again. We go deeper into the jungle than we have before and the road is more pitted. I bounce and dust swirls around my head, making my coughing even worse. I wrap my scarf tightly around my throat and mouth.

Then Ajay raises his hand. Sudhir pulls over and turns off the engine. And again that silence that is this jungle. For a few moments they whisper, then they are quiet again. If they are not talking, they are listening. Sometimes it seems they hear something because they point their fingers into the air. They cock their heads to see if this is an alarm call or just some ordinary animal sound. Ajay tries to help me hear whatever he does. He has spent his life learning to tell the differences among all these sounds that escape me. "Do you hear this, Mary?" he asks me over and over again. Wild chickens, wild boar rutting, white-tailed deer calling to her young. Peacocks calling to assemble. "No tiger." Ajay shakes his head.

I try to listen, but I don't hear a thing.

47

I'M THE CHILD of a deaf man. My father had scarlet fever as a boy and lost most of his hearing. It is difficult talking to him and worse when he talks to us. Actually he never talks. He shouts. He barks. My mother likes to joke that his bark is worse than his bite, but that brought me little consolation. He is an angry man, angry in ways I'll never understand, but even if he isn't angry, he sounds that way. Everything in our house is loud. The TV, music, dinner talk. As I grow older, I develop an aversion to noise.

When I'm sixteen, my father has ear surgery. I'm not sure I understand it, but it is discussed in our house for a long time. Would he have it? Wouldn't he? But he does. Afterward he's in a lot of pain. And he doesn't seem to hear any better than he did before. But then one day when I'm at a friend's, my mother calls. Would you like to talk to your father on the phone? she asks.

I say sure, why not. And then as I hear his voice I realize that I've never talked to him on the phone before. He couldn't really hear. When I get home, they tell me what happened. My mother was walking through the room and suddenly my father jumped, startled. What's that? He asked her. And my mother stopped walking. What's what? It was her footsteps. He'd never heard footsteps. At last he can hear them. But the thing I'd hoped the surgery would fix doesn't work. He never stops shouting.

My father's temper is a family secret. Later, when I tell people about it, they are stunned. One cousin refuses to believe me. It doesn't seem possible that the charming man they knew was capable of such rage. But there is a Yiddish phrase for this: "Street angel, house devil." Once, when he is quite old, my father is driving with my mother, and a friend of theirs is in the car. The woman says something, no one seems to remember what it was, and my father lights into her. He calls her the worst kind of person, a liar, a piece of garbage. I can't remember it all, but what I remember is my mother's response. She comes home beside herself, in tears, and tells me how stunned she is. "This never happened before," she says.

I am dumbstruck by her response. "Yes, it did, Mom. It happened every night."

"But it never happened with people before," she replies.

Over the years friends tell me how brave I am. How

they admire my courage. I have no idea what they mean. I see nothing courageous in anything I do. I feel safer on a mountain pass, in the snake-infested jungle, or sleeping on a straw mat in some funky border town than I ever did at home.

48

A GROWN TIGER can weigh up to six hundred pounds and, as a species, has been hunting for more than two million years. And it has memory. A tiger remembers slights and grudges. It has its enemies. In John Vaillant's brilliant nonfiction book, simply called *The Tiger*, an Amur tiger in northern Siberia stalks and kills a man named Vladimir Markov specifically for the purpose of revenge. This is not a spoiler; the reader learns this on the first page.

Markov knew that he was being stalked and that there was little he could do to stop it. When his remains are found, or what little is left of him, an official involved in the case asked out loud, "Why is the tiger so angry?"

49

Brooklyn, 2008

EVERY MORNING Larry draws my bath. I lie in bed sipping coffee or reading the paper until it is ready. I hop on one leg on the upstairs walker into the bathroom. The room is steamy hot, the mirrors cloud up. Larry tests the temperature with his elbow—the way I did for our daughter when she was small. He places the shampoo, conditioner, soap, and washcloth along the side of the tub. "Okay," he'll say. "I think we're ready." I make my way to the side of the tub, drop my robe, as Larry pulls out two plastic trash bags and begins the arduous process of wrapping my leg. He ties the bags tightly around my thigh, securing it with duct tape.

He waits as I swivel from the side of the tub onto the white plastic chair that sits inside. I rest my leg on the side of the tub, then ease my way into the water as Larry pulls away the chair. I soak, careful to keep my leg raised. My days used to begin with a walk in the park or a morning swim. I'd write until midafternoon, and then meet a friend for coffee or a drink at a nearby café. On the way home I'd shop for dinner. I'd put on some music as I stood at the counter, chopping vegetables, peeling shrimp. Now this seems far away.

Each day is excruciatingly the same. I wash, then call Larry to help me out of the tub. On the edge I dry myself. While I'm dressing, Larry goes downstairs. He prepares my breakfast and my lunch. Then he rinses the commode we keep by the bed (because I can't get to the bathroom in the night). It had never occurred to me that this would be part of our marital contract—the sickness-and-health part that we'd agreed to. But he never complains. He never shirks. His last task of the morning is to carry the commode down to the supply closet in my office, where he's made a space.

There's a bathroom on the ground level, but the hallway is too narrow. I can't get my walker through. So I keep the blinds in my office drawn and when I need to, hop over to the commode. At the end of the day he empties it.

The pain surprises me. I didn't anticipate it. It's different from any other pain I've known. I've had nerve pain, I've had muscle pain. But this one comes from deep inside my bones. It is especially bad at night for some reason. I take whatever painkillers I am allowed, but it is never enough. Every night I find myself shivering. The only thing I can do is pull the caramel-colored blanket over my head. I disappear under the covers, sometimes for hours at a time. I don't know why, but this seems to help. Larry, my optimistic husband, says that it must be the pain of the bone healing. Like growing pains. But this feels like the opposite. Every night it feels as if I am shattering all over again.

A week after my accident, Larry returns to work. The flowers stop coming and the visits grow sporadic. The novelty of my broken leg begins to wear off. The days are an endless routine—each beginning and ending in the same way. But that first Sunday is the worst because Larry, a journalist, always works on Sundays. As well as often on holidays such as Thanksgiving or Christmas. I never liked it, but it's his job. Still he felt badly, leaving me that first

Sunday. I could see it in his eyes. That day I never make it down to my office. I just sit on our sofa, watching families heading off to brunch. I cry. I try to hide this from my husband. For most of the day I don't answer the phone. People think I am resting.

50

ON OCTOBER 3, 2003, at the Mirage in Las Vegas, Chris Lawrence knew something was wrong. He was one of the chief animal handlers for the team of magicians and performers known as Siegfried and Roy, and he worked with Mantecore, the tiger, every day. And Mantecore was not responding to Roy Horn's commands. Murmurs rose from the crew backstage. The tiger was going rogue, but before they could do anything, the four-hundred-pound beast wrapped his jaws around Roy's neck and dragged him offstage. At first the audience of fifteen hundred thought this was part of the act. An illusion concocted by the Masters of the Impossible. Slowly they realized it was not.

The official version of the story is that Roy had a stroke onstage and the tiger was trying to protect him, but in fact the opposite is true. Roy's stroke occurred as a result of the attack. Years later Chris Lawrence broke his silence. He said that for months before the attack Roy had stopped feeding the tigers and stopped whispering to them before their shows. In other words Roy broke the bond and the tiger felt no loyalty to comply. The animal handlers and crew tried to distract Mantecore, but in the end the tiger simply released Roy and walked away.

51

India, 2011

I'M GROWING ACCUSTOMED to the rhythm of our days. The predawn knock on the door. The stinging cold. The tray of tea and biscuits. Our drive to the preserve, where we bribe a guide, and Ajay swings into the jeep. On day three, he removes the scarf for the first time. It is as if he doesn't mind my seeing him. His hair is slick and wet. Clearly he has showered. I feel as if in some way I am being honored, but I'm too cold and sick to care. I now have two hot-water bottles—one provided by the hotel. One is in my lap and another at my feet. I have blankets over me and I can't stop coughing. I know that I have a respiratory infection deep in my chest. I'm fairly certain it's not contagious, but I'm as sick as a dog. I'm just hoping it isn't pneumonia. I should see a doctor, but that will have to wait. And I have no antibiotics.

Dawn is breaking as we drive into the park. A family of monkeys greets us before they scatter through the trees. I laugh, watching them go. A jackal peers from the side of the road, waiting for us to drive by. We go a bit farther, then stop at a crossroads. Spotted deer graze in the distance, steam rising with their breath. It is here that I miss my daughter, Kate, the most. We have shared our love of animals—the iguanas that lived on the roof of the beach hut we rented in Costa Rica, the sea turtle she swam with in the Caymans, the sea lion that played chicken with her in the Galápagos. She would love this, and I make a vow to bring her here one day. Maybe when she has children of her own.

For now we pause as Ajay does what he does best—listen. His eyes dart through the brush as Sudhir watches him, listening too. After a few moments Ajay points to the right, and we head off. I have no idea what he has heard, but I trust his instincts. I know he is a good man—the same way, perhaps, that Larry knew that Dr. Patel was a good surgeon. You feel something about people at times. And I felt it here. We are driving on a road on the far right side of the reserve. I haven't been down this road and it is more rutted, and, therefore, less traveled.

In a tree above we see a snake-eating hawk. Sudhir hates snake-eating hawks. But it is beautiful to see that bird above us. Other birds dart by and Ajay can name them all—even if he doesn't see them. He knows them by their songs and by the flapping of their wings. We stop again and Ajay raises his finger into the air. He reminds me of a friend of mine who, just from a few bars, can name any Duke Ellington song—including when and where it was recorded and even what take.

"Do you hear that?" Sudhir whispers. I shake my head. "Listen," he says.

I listen and then I do hear something. A very high-pitched squeal. It is barely audible and seems as if it is coming from miles away. "Yes, I do hear that."

"Barking deer calling spotted deer alarm call."

Once more we are off at breakneck speed on this deeply pitted road, driving into terrain where no other tourists come. We drive across a narrow riverbed, our wheels underwater. We drive past a ghost tree—its pure white branches reaching overhead. At last we come to a savanna of tall grass, rimmed by the forest. We stop and Ajay stands up. His eyes scan the borders of the savanna. He is looking for a flicker in the grass, a movement that isn't the wind but a large beast making her way. He reads the forest the way fishermen read the sea. He knows every ripple, what every bent blade of grass might mean. "She's in there," he says with confidence. "She's lying down. She's out there," Ajay says. He points to the bushes where in fact I can see the slight rustle in the grass. I ask him how he knows that it's a "she."

This is when I learn that all unseen tigers are referred to as she. He doesn't know why. Perhaps because they are mysterious and unpredictable like hurricanes. This will also be true when I push on to Kahna. Later I will learn that even in the most remote parts of Siberia where the Amur tiger roams, the unseen tiger is "she." Good trackers can tell from the pugmarks if it is a male or female, but if you have not seen her or her mark, then it is she.

The tiger has been around for more than two million years. Humans have always known the tiger. In Asia there is no place in memory that a tiger does not roam. In the jungles of India or the taiga of Siberia, what lurks out there, what you can hear breathing as if you are the one being hunted, is she.

We are parked at the edge of a river with savanna around us. White-tailed deer, sambar deer, wild boar graze in the open meadows. Aquatic birds wade in the bulrushes. Clearly they do not sense any danger nearby. Ajay's eyes are on the dry brush at the edge of the savanna. He listens for the cries and watches for any movement in the grass. "She's in the bush," he says. "She's out there."

52

Brooklyn, 2008

ON THE DAYS when I go to see Dr. Patel, I try to look my best. I wear blue sweaters and earrings to accent my eyes. Lipstick, hair blown dry. The works. A visit to the doctor is a major event in my otherwise uneventful world. It's as if I'm auditioning for a role. The role of perfect patient. I begin to fantasize about Dr. Patel. Not in an intimate, sexual way. It's more the way I once fantasized over my seventh-grade teacher. I want to know about him and his life. I try to get information out of him. I understand this is a common occurrence. I had a friend once who, after an accident, had a long affair with her plastic surgeon who was married and many years her senior.

From the moment Dr. Patel walked into my hospital room at four in the morning in his green scrubs, I was drawn to this man. He was going to be my savior. I don't know if there is the medical equivalent of Stockholm syndrome, but I think I had a case of it. I am the kidnapped, identifying with my captor. I am Patty Hearst to his Symbionese Liberation Army. My foot, my freedom, it is all in his hands. I have to believe that he is the best and I need to believe that I matter to him. Of course there are transient relationships in this world that are intended to be transient. Teacher to student, architect to client, doctor to patient. And yet at the time when we are living within their sphere, they can become the most important person of all.

I befriend his assistant, Naomi. She is young and quite attractive with long, dark hair. I imagine that she and Dr. Patel are a couple. That they have a thing, but it's an office secret. I envision her lingering after work, waiting for him to take her out for a drink. Do they sit in dark corners of restaurants, eating steak? One day when Naomi is standing in his office, she tells me that she had an ankle injury similar to mine, only from a car wreck. Her ankle is filled with hardware. She's wearing high heels. Something I can't imagine ever wearing again. I admire her scar and her shoes.

One afternoon when he is running particularly late, I ask her, "So what's his story?"

Naomi gives me a sly look. "What do you mean?"

"I mean, you know, is he married or what?"

Naomi confides in me that nobody knows. He is a very private person. This only feeds my fantasies more. I don't want to sleep with my doctor. But I want him to know me when I'm not laid up. When my life bears a semblance of what it had been before. I imagine inviting him over for dinner. He can bring Naomi. But he comes alone. He brings a good bottle of red wine and gives me a kiss on the cheek. He shakes Larry's hand and meets Kate. They joke about "her mom," and he thinks she's a great girl. He drinks scotch and compliments the food. He becomes my friend.

Except for visits to the doctor and the occasional morning coffee I'm a shut-in. Friends come by. They sit on my sofa, chatting. I'm a captive audience, a priest at the confessional, the therapist they've always wanted. Many share the secrets of their lives—things they've never told me before. One confides that she's thinking of ending her marriage. (She does.) Another tells me that she fears her daughter is doing drugs. (She's not.) Still, this doesn't stave off my feelings of imprisonment.

I read the opening of Naguib Mahfouz's novel *Palace Walk*. A woman, staring down at the street, recalls passing the market below on her way to the house where she was to live after her wedding. That was thirty years ago, and she has not been outside since. How do women all over the world do this? Women in harems, shut-ins who are stuck at home or who, for whatever reason, cannot leave. I put the book down. I can barely breathe.

Depression settles in. I google dreary stories. Virgin found in trash. Man commits suicide after putting his dog down. When I read about the Puerto Rican grandmother in the Bronx, murdered by a person posing as a wheelchair trainer, I weep.

53

India, 2008

SUDHIR LOVES SNAKES. He loves to capture them and set them free. If they sneak into your house, then, Sudhir tells me, happily, I am your man. Back in his room at the hotel where he stays, he has an eight-foot male python that crawled into the house of one of the villagers, probably because of the cold. "Snakes don't like the cold." Sudhir says he's looking for a female python. He wants them to mate. Then he'll set them free back into the wild. Sudhir talks a blue streak. Back at the hotel he asks me if I'd like to see his python and I tell him I would, not really sure of what this might entail. In another context this would be a pickup line.

Shortly after lunch Sudhir drags a huge gunnysack onto the lawn and dumps the python in front of me. "That crawled into somebody's house?" I am in shock.

Sudhir smiles, proud of himself, as he caresses the snake's head. The snake begins to coil around Sudhir's arm, working its way toward his neck, until Sudhir decides that this isn't such a great idea, and for the next fifteen minutes, he struggles to stuff the snake back into the gunnysack. He'll get a midsection in and the head comes out. Then vice versa. It's clearly easier to get the snake out of the sack than it is to shove it back.

54

India, 2011

THAT AFTERNOON there's no tiger safari planned. I am offered a ride in a bullock cart instead, but I opt out of that. I want to visit some of the nearby villages. I'm happy to do it on foot, but Sudhir has offered to take me. It only occurs to me in hindsight that walking around isn't encouraged when you're only miles from a tiger reserve with no buffer zone. I'm assuming we'll tool around a little and stop off along the way.

But this is not what the hotel or Sudhir thinks is proper for a person of my stature, not to mention for their only guest—and one they'd prefer to see go home alive. I arrive at the edge of the property at about four and see that Sudhir has the jeep, stocked with water and hats, and there are servants waiting to help me on board. Not what I had in mind, but I don't have the heart to disappoint or embarrass him after he'd been so nice, showing me his python.

In the jeep are a few other people, all local. Perhaps we are taking them to their villages. A young girl sits beside me. As we go along the dusty, potholed road, she keeps smiling at me but is silent. I'm assuming she's from a village and we'll drop her off along the way. We drive through one village, then another, but we don't seem to be stopping. We pass another village with houses with thatched roofs, and I want to stop, but Sudhir tells me that we will later. It seems there is an itinerary. This is a guided tour. Definitely not what I'd had in mind.

We pass through towns where men and women, stooped in the fields, are doing backbreaking work. In the rice paddies children plow with their bullocks. In the dusty streets of a town they play a game with a battered plastic water bottle and a stick. Nothing is paved. There is dust everywhere. In a patch of shade, a woman with long nails and hennaed hands works at separating the rice from the chaff. A bullock walks in circles, turning a grinding stone. The woman wraps her yellow sari around her face. I put my hands together in greeting and she bows her head.

In the past week I've been in planes, cars, jeeps for days, and what I really want is to walk around. To see how people live in the villages, but Sudhir is hesitant to stop. In the jeep the girl is more or less silent the whole ride. Finally, I put my foot down. "I need to walk," I tell him. He seems miffed, not really understanding. For Sudhir, I know, this is a big honor, driving me through the towns. But I'd prefer less of an honor. "Please," I ask him, "can't we just walk around?"

"But there are more interesting villages a few miles ahead." I actually don't care about the more interesting villages. I am happy to visit one of these. I was hoping to leave my hotel and wander around, but apparently that's not possible. We push on farther along the rutted road until I don't think I can take being bounced and jostled any longer. I point to a village on a hill. "Why don't we just stop there?"

Sudhir points. "You want to stop there?"

"Why not?"

I can tell he's disappointed. There must be a village some distance from here that he wants to show me, but between my throat and coughing and the dust and the bumpy road I don't think I can go on. We stop at a dry riverbed and park the jeep. When I get out, I'm wobbly, as if I've been on a horse all day. I don't think I've stretched my legs since I arrived in India. And the truth is, even hardly walking, my ankle feels sore. I'm longing to test it. There is only one road going through the village and I follow it. And in a matter of moments the word is out that there is a visitor.

Children pop out of doorways. Women, saris pulled over their heads, greet me as I pass, hands pressed together in the usual "Namaste" greeting. At first, I try just smiling, but they look away so I repeat the "Namaste" greeting. Sudhir walks beside me and shares with me some of his own story. He has a wife and child who live back in Nagpur, which is about six hours away. He goes home a couple of times a year or they come to visit him here. "I want my wife to move down here, but she doesn't want to leave her family," he says. "We argue about that."

"My husband moved to America from Canada."

"We have to make sacrifices. Anyway, my work is here."

We walk on in silence for a while as village children peer out from houses made of straw and wooden slats with dirt floors. In front, women sweep with short brooms, but it all seems a fairly useless endeavor to keep the dust out of the dirt. Young girls walk with plastic jugs on their heads to and from the well. There seems to be no running water or electricity, but then suddenly in the middle of the village, in front of a house, a sewing machine appears. It looks brand-new and sitting at it is a woman in a pale blue sari, its gossamer fabric blowing in the dust and the wind, as she hems a cuff on a pair of pants with her foot working the pedal.

Seeing her there, so incongruous, head bowed, working away, is striking. Later in New York, when I go to my local appliance store, I will learn about the sewing-machine project. My neighborhood store contributes dozens of sewing machines a year to villages in India to provide women with a means of employment. This woman has stacks of trousers and saris in a basket at her feet, waiting for her to mend them. We walk on to the edge of the town, where I gaze across the rice paddies and wheat fields. Women in green and crimson and blue saris work in the fields. "All right," I tell Sudhir, "let's head back."

We get in the jeep and start the ride back. The girl is still with us. I'd assumed that Sudhir is taking her to her village, but that doesn't seem to be the case. On the way back she and I start talking with Sudhir translating, as the girl has only a few words of English. He explains that she is just along for the ride. "No clients at hotel. Just sightseeing," he tells me, and the girl smiles at me, her head bobbing.

She is the hotel masseuse. She laughs at the thought that she is from a village nearby. Her name is Asha and she comes from the south, from Kerala. She has taken a three-month massage training course. She holds up three fingers. Three months doesn't seem like a lot of training, but perhaps that's customary here. "Have massage?"

Anyway, I think, "Why not?" The girl can probably use the business. At the worst it will be another cultural experience. And the cost is negligible. Three hundred rupees, she assures me. Only about four dollars. I ask three times and she assures me. Three hundred rupees. I agree to meet her at the massage house at eight o'clock.

55

SARAH BERNHARDT traveled with a tiger on a leash. It
was rumored that her tiger once devoured two waiters
in an American restaurant. She went to Paris with her
tiger, passing it off as "a spotted African cat" because the
manager of the Paris hotel had heard about the incident
in America. Apparently Bernhardt kept her exotic pet in
order to distract people from the fact that she was Jewish. She wanted people to think of her as just being crazy
and wild. The solitude and wildness of the tiger reaches
into our most primitive selves. Perhaps they are a reminder
of another time when we too roamed free. Instead of tied
down as we are by time and space, by mortgages and jobs
and family obligations. A friend's child recently asked his
father, "Why do humans live in captivity?" My friend was
at a loss for words.

56

I'M AT A LECTURE in Mumbai about tiger conservation,
and a woman asks the naturalist if keeping a tiger as a pet
would help in their preservation. And the naturalist, who
can barely hide his disdain, replies, "No, madam, it would
not help. And tigers do not make good pets."

57

Brooklyn, 2008

MY VISITING NURSE—a dour man—shows up unannounced about a week after I get home. I'm surprised when he rings the bell and have no idea who he is. "I've been assigned to your case," he tells me as I open the door. This troubles me since I didn't know I am or have a case. Still I let him in, and he puts me through the motions like a trained seal. He has me hop on my good leg, propelling myself with a walker across my carpeted office floor. He scribbles notes on a pad, says very little, except to tell me that he's requisitioning a wheelchair, which arrives a few days later. To Larry's relief it comes fully assembled. He just has to sign for it.

From the start I have a bad relationship with the wheelchair. It is heavy and cumbersome. It's a struggle to get the footrests in place. I hate the way it bounces over the bumpy sidewalk, the curbs. Tree roots are enemies. I don't like being three feet off the ground, eye level with babies in strollers. And though this, of course, is ridiculous in retrospect, it seems as if this chair has a personality of its own—somewhat contemptuous, disapproving. An "I told you so" look to its stolid, stubborn frame. And it terrifies me. I feel as if I have no control over what is happening. I'm not unlike a baby in this regard. Babies are born with only one natural fear. That is the fear of falling. If you put a baby on a glass table, it will start scrambling and shriek-ing. It doesn't know that a layer of glass stands between it and the abyss.

As Larry pushes me along the street in my wheelchair, I try to explain this to him. I tell him that from my vantage point it looks as if the FreshDirect truck is going to run me over. No matter how much he reassures me, I can't quite believe that a van hurtling along the avenue is going to see me, so low to the ground, in time to stop.

And it makes me feel old. Is this what it's going to be like? I ask myself. In twenty, thirty years? Being in it reminds me of my parents, late in their lives. My father particularly. How he despised the indignity of being carted around. The last time I saw my father, he was grip-ping his walker, banging it through the apartment. He was determined to beat death. He'd do it with these steps. My father, an avid walker, tried walking until the bitter end.

A few days after the wheelchair arrives, my ever-patient husband is wheeling me to a store when a neighborhood Muslim boy who lives above the dry cleaner stops to speak to me. "What happened to you?" he asks. This boy is para-lyzed, his body twisted in an odd way, and I've watched him grow up in a wheelchair since he was very young. Yet this is the first time he's ever said a word to me. For once we are eye-to-eye. And I tell him that I've had a bad fall.

"So you'll get better, right?" he asks, somewhat disap-pointed, I think.

"I hope so," I reply.

He nods, dropping his head. "I hope so too. My name is Ibrahim. I was born this way. But I'm only paralyzed from the waist down. My arms are strong." He flexes a muscle to show me. Then he spins with his front wheels off the ground and bounces up a tall curb. Larry gives him a thumbs-up and I try to smile, wondering if I'll be popping wheelies soon as well.

Six months later, when I'm walking, I'll see Ibrahim again at a block party. I'll hobble up to him on my cane and say, "Hello, Ibrahim."

He'll look up at me oddly, "How do you know my name?"

58

India, 2011

THAT EVENING after dinner I make my way through the woods. Perhaps a good massage will get my energy flowing again. Besides, I feel sorry for the girl. There was something sad and shy about her. I trip over something on the path. A root perhaps. I can't really tell. Jungle sounds pierce the darkness. Birds or monkeys. Nothing threatening. Certainly not tigers. No predators roam this far from the reserve—though there are packs of feral dogs.

I follow the path though it's difficult to tell in the dark just which direction the massage house is. I hope I'm not lost. In the daylight it had made more sense, but now I'm not sure. It should be right beside the pool, but the path isn't lit. I stumble on a large rock, then walk right into a cable that secures a tent. Ahead, the blue lights of the pool shine. And past the pool is a stone cottage. Up several steps a silhouette is framed in a doorway.

At the entrance the girl is waiting for me, and right away I can tell that she's trembling, rubbing her arms and trying to get warm. She's wearing only the same thin cotton dress she had on during the day, but now the sun is gone. The massage building itself is just bare cinder block, no curtains or rugs. I am sure that there must be some kind of space heater or secluded massage room inside.

But there isn't. It's just as cold inside as it is outside, and I wince under the bright fluorescent light. Asha has put clean towels down on the massage table and plucked petals from the bougainvillea vine that grows on the wall outside. She's arranged them in a special pattern she learned in school. But I can see my breath. Since the sun went down, it's as if a blanket of ice has been laid across the forest. I'm thinking about walking back to my cottage. This is more like a place for interrogation than the spa I'd been hoping for. There's no scent of candles, no soft music. In fact, there is nothing here that feels even remotely relaxing. Surely there's some other room, some secret place where the girl will guide me and a heater will be on. They can't do a massage here. As she touches me, I'm stunned. Her hands are freezing; it's as if death is touching me.

I am wondering if I can get out of this massage grace-fully when a man arrives. He's dressed in a camouflage jacket and a woolen cap. But as he rubs his mittened hands together, I know I've seen him around the hotel. The other day he approached me after my morning safari. I thought he was being friendly, but he was just trying to drum up business. Then he was dressed in a T-shirt and jeans because in the light of day it is warm in this valley of hibiscus and lemons. I'd taken a dislike to him and I'm not pleased to see him now.

He thrusts a piece of paper in a plastic binder into my face. I don't know what it is, then I look again, and I'm stunned. It is the list of services and prices. The massage is ten times what Asha told me in the jeep. Pointing, I shake my head. A full massage is three thousand rupees. Not the three hundred the girl repeated at least twice in the jeep. "No," I say, "no, no, no. Too expensive." I look at Asha. "This is not what you said."

The girl laughs a nervous laugh. She needs this mas-sage. There is no one else at the hotel and she probably hasn't worked in days. While I realize that working here is a pretty good job for her, she probably has to pay for her room and board. And the behavior of this man seems to indicate as much. Still it is ten times more than she said it would be. I'm scanning the price list. "Shoulder massage, full-body massage, pressure massage . . ."

The girl seems desperate. Anyone can see that. The beg-gars banging tin pots or pointing to their hungry children, those dark pleading eyes, the old ladies selling marigold garlands, it seems as if everyone is hustling just to get to their next meal. Even the animals. Those skinny sacred cows who wander through the cities (and with all these people starving). And the mangy dogs. Yesterday at the hotel I tossed a bone toward a dog crouched in the bushes, and in seconds a pack of dogs were going at one another's throats. So the girl needs the money, and what is it really to me? Forty dollars instead of four. I'd pay twice that for dinner in Manhattan.

Finally, I agree. Just head and shoulders, forty minutes, 1,200 rupees. "Good deal," Asha says. She takes me by a trembling hand. "You come with me. Massage." The girl leads me behind a screen where the light is just as harsh and the room just as cold. "Perhaps if we shut the front door," I say, but again the girl shakes her head. I stare at the wooden massage table, a single green towel strewn with pink petals. "Come." The girl points to my chest. "Take off clothes."

On the other side of the screen the man is pacing. I'd expected some privacy. A fluffy towel to cover myself. But none is offered. Asha wants me to get undressed. Just take off my clothes in front of her, with a strange man pacing on the other side. I refuse. I can't.

The girl tugs at my shirt and jacket. "Take off."

I want to leave. I want to run out of here. "No," I say, hands folded across my chest like a petulant child.

Asha looks at me oddly. At last with a sigh I take off my

jacket and sweatshirt. I leave on my shirt, my loose-fitting
pants. But at least I'm taking off something. I lie on the
cold metal table as if I'm waiting for my own autopsy. I
rub myself with my hands. In the corner Asha is trying
to warm the oil with a candle. I realize that while she has
sprinkled bougainvillea petals on the table and the floor,
she forgot to heat up the oil. She comes over and begins to
pour it on my head.

The oil is cold and I'm still not sure if I have hot water
in my cottage. I haven't had a hot shower since I arrived
at this jungle camp, and I have no idea how I'll be able to
wash the oil out. But what can I do? The girl is already
rubbing in the oil, more the way a mother puts baby lotion
on a child's bottom than an actual massage. "You good?
Everything all right?" Asha asks. She keeps running her
fingers through my hair. I'm waiting for the massage to
begin.

"Yes," I reply. "Everything is all right."

As the girl runs her fingers through the oil, then adds
more, I realize that this is my massage. It has begun. I suppose I could get up and go, but I won't. I'm already in, so
I may as well grit my teeth and be nice about it. I gesture
to the girl to wait a moment as I unbutton my blouse. No
point getting oil all over everything. And, since there is
nothing to be done, and since I don't want the girl to have
trouble with her boss, I try and make conversation if only
to pass the time. "How long have you been here?"

"I here four months. Very cold."

"Yes," I say, "very cold." The girl is scratching my scalp. "You can go deeper," I say. "You won't hurt me." But she shrugs, laughs, and keeps on scratching. "So why did you come here?" I ask. Of course, I know the answer. Because work is here. But I don't want to just say it. And perhaps a conversation would do us both good.

"Mother, brother. Need money."

"So you send money home?" Asha pours oil on my neck, slopping it onto my skin. Her cold hands slick tepid oil over my shoulders and neck, and I tremble as she does so.

"Yes, mother only two hundred rupees a week. Father dead. I work."

"Oh," I say, now feeling worse for the girl. "I am sorry to hear that." Her hands graze my body. "Can you go deeper?" She nods, grinning, but like an aquatic bird Asha only skims the surface of my skin.

"Yes, father. Heart attack." The girl points to her heart. She makes a gesture as if she is falling over dead, though for some reason she is smiling.

"I'm so sorry," I say. "My father too died . . . not that long ago. How old was he?"

The girl holds up her fingers. "Thirty-four," the girl says, once more laughing. I can't comprehend this laughter. Is it a cultural thing? To laugh about sadness? Is it something only Buddhists can understand? The circle of life. The need to let go. Part of her belief system? The girl is laughing because to her the universe is funny. Another shiver goes through me.

"Ah." The girl laughs again. "We same." She points to me, then to her own heart. Once more she's pushing the oil up and down my shoulders and back.

"Deeper," I ask. Asha nods and keeps doing the same thing.

She goes to work on my neck. She puts her hands around my throat. "Yes," she goes on. "It was sudden." Her hands still haven't warmed, and she keeps trembling. In the main room the man is pacing.

I close my eyes, wishing I could drift off. Just fall asleep on this hard table in this cold room, but I can't. For years I've barely slept without the help of pills. "Designer sleep," I call it. I don't dream when I take pills. I used to have nightmares all the time. That's why the night frightened me. I'm in a forest or walking in a meadow. A snowy field. I come upon a path and, no matter which way I go, it always brings me back to my childhood home. A place I spent decades escaping. Always when I arrive, I'm a little girl again. It is winter and I'm standing alone in the snow.

Asha steps back. "Massage done."

I drag myself off the table. My breasts feel heavy, my limbs stiffer than they were before it began. My head is anointed with oil. Shaking, I slip into my clothes. Asha turns away, pretending to straighten the room. When I'm dressed, I hand her a hundred rupees as a tip, which she pockets into her dress, though in moments I'm sure the man will take it from her. As I leave the massage building, someone calls. "Excuse me, excuse me, miss." It is the man. I must sign the voucher. I go back and look at the voucher. Nothing is written on it. "This is blank," I say to the man.

"Will fill in later," he tells me. I sign my name, then stagger out into the forest. It is colder and darker than it was before.

Overhead the sky is illumined with a million stars. There are creatures out here. I hear them. The rustling of the bushes, calls. And other things I now believe. Ghosts. India has its ghosts. But now I don't feel as if something is out there, watching me. I feel as if it doesn't even matter that I'm here. In the darkness I trip over a tent wire, catching myself just before I fall; then I rush back to the cottage, where I turn on the shower.

I stand, waiting for the shower to warm up, but it doesn't. I can't believe that my head is covered in oil and I don't have any warm water to wash it. I am furious now and wrap a towel around my head, race to the main house, where I begin to complain. I'm sick, I'm freezing, and my head is covered in oil. The manager sends a worker to my room who fiddles with the valves. Immediately hot water pours out of the shower.

It is then that I notice that the hot and cold are switched. It says "hot" for cold. And "cold" for hot. Later the manager will apologize. "Someone should have explained that to you." Apparently, they are switched throughout the hotel.

59

Brooklyn, 2008

ONE MORNING when Larry draws my bath, I am in a particularly bad mood. It is almost the day when I would have been leaving for Morocco. I should be packing, checking my camera, buying a new journal. Instead I'm struggling to get into a tub of hot water. Larry tries to help me, but I resist. "I can do it myself," I tell him. Instead I manage to slip and my injured leg dips into the water, soaking my bandage. At first, I don't worry about it. It will dry, I tell myself, but several hours later the wound starts to itch, and I call Larry at work. "I think I need to go to the hospital and get this bandage changed," I tell him.

I call a friend and she takes me over. I keep apologizing because there's a wait but there's nothing I can do, and she is a good sport. It takes more than an hour for them to see me and the attendant tells me they'll have to unwrap and rebandage my leg. I sit calmly as they start to remove the yards and yards, or so it seems, of gauze. My friend and I joke. It's like a magic trick gone wrong. At last, when it is removed, I see my foot for the first time. Except this thing cannot be my foot. And now it's not funny at all. This is a monster's foot, a cadaver's limb. This foot cannot connect to any living being or living tissue, and certainly not to my body. It is green and mangled, swollen beyond recognition. Surely this is not my foot. I start to sob, and the nurse shakes her head. My friend pats my back. Nothing they can do will comfort me. This is a limb from a bad movie, a horror film, an alien's appendage, one I wish I'd never seen.

60

NO TWO TIGERS have the same stripes. They are as distinct as human faces, as snowflakes. No two are alike. Their stripes are their fingerprint. And they are symmetrical. It is like that child's art assignment when you put paint on a piece of paper and fold it in two. A Rorschach test. Do you see the bat or the ballerina? The clown or the vase? This is how they count tigers in the wild. They identify them by their stripes.

Ajay knows one tiger from the next and he knows the lineage of every tiger in the park. He can recite their ancestors the way we refer to our own. If he sees a tiger, he immediately knows it by its stripes. He recognizes them just as we recognize our friends and acquaintances by their faces. He knows their mothers, their siblings, and sometimes even their sires. None are strangers to him. He has given them all names.

61

India, 2011

THE NEXT MORNING after I bribe the usual guides Ajay gets into our jeep. But he seems glum. He barely says hello. His wife's pink scarf almost entirely obscures his face. He even ignores Sudhir's endless banter in Hindi. At first, I think there's something wrong at home. Perhaps he's worried how he will feed another child. But then I sense it is not about anything personal. It's about the tiger. The tiger eludes him.

I've come to recognize Ajay's moods. At times he seems confident and assured. He is a man who has, after all, tracked hundreds, if not thousands, of tigers in his years as a naturalist. He is perhaps not much more than thirty years old, but he is regarded, at least by Sudhir, as one of the best guides in all of India. And yet we have not seen a single sign, heard a single roar, even an alarm call. It is a point of pride for Ajay but in some ways the tiger has become less important to me. I have come on this journey alone. I am doing what I wanted to do—even if I don't see a tiger.

We drive around for two hours, stopping when a jackal comes out of the woods, when a herd of young deer saunters by. But not once does Ajay raise his finger for Sudhir to stop. Not once does he seem to hear what I thus far have been unable to hear. Those distant cries that signal that a tiger may be near.

We stop for lunch at Alikatta and in a circle of sun munch on cheese sandwiches and peel oranges. Nearby the elephants, tugging on their chains, eat their huge chapatis. Then we get back in our jeep and, without a word, we're on our way.

62

BY NATURE a tiger is not a man-eater. We are not part of her normal diet. We are more of an acquired taste. They say that if a tiger threatens you, unless you can climb a tree, stand up very tall. *Homo erectus* is not prey to the tiger. It attacks creatures on four legs. This is why it tends to attack workers in the field. They are often crouched and mistaken for antelope or deer. This is why some workers have faces tattooed on the backs of their heads. So that if the tiger is about to attack, it will see a human face.

63

Brooklyn, 2008

SIX WEEKS into my disability I look up from my desk to see a face smashed against the window. It looks like a freaky mask, but it turns out to be my friend Maria. She's standing at the window with a basket in her hand, trying to see if I'm at my desk. I'm a bit of a sitting duck because my ground-floor office faces the street. Anyone can see if I am working. But to open the door is a chore. I have to get my walker, hop to the door, open it, hop back. Same thing when the friend leaves. It all seems like too much effort. But there is Maria with her face pressed to my window and picnic basket in hand.

She's brought me bread, wine, some cheese, and salami. "Let's pretend we're in France," she says as she spreads a checkered tablecloth across my desk. Hard as I try not to, I find myself growing annoyed and sad. I don't want to pretend I'm in France. I want to be in France. "You'll see," she says to me, "someday, a year from now, five years from now, or even later, or sooner, you'll see the secret gift in all of this."

The secret gift? And now I am furious at Maria for ambushing me (even with a French picnic basket) and then suggesting that there can be some good outcome from all of this. What secret gift can there be? I think of all the terrible things that have happened to people throughout history. Was there a secret gift in concentration camps and pogroms? In the 9/11 terrorist attacks? If my husband's plane crashes, what is the secret gift there? The only thing I can see as a blessing is that I won't have to visit my mother for a while. I have a perfect excuse.

When my father died three years earlier, my mother and I had a real falling out. I would have to say that I lost both of my parents at once. I didn't blame my mother for not mourning my father's passing. They'd had a rough marriage, and, for all his good looks and charm, he was a difficult man. I always thought she should have left him years ago, but as she once said to me, "That wasn't done." Her marriage was her own business, but I couldn't forgive her for showing no compassion to me in my grief.

At his memorial service, which I arrange, she complains that it is taking too long. She hates the fact that there are prayers. Over lunch she turns to me and asks, "What's wrong, Mary? You look tired." She doesn't want his ashes so I receive them. Actually, FedEx delivers them to the chiropractor next door when I'm not home. When the chiropractor calls, I ask him if it's from Bed Bath & Beyond, as I was expecting a delivery of towels. "Well," he replies awkwardly, "it's from beyond."

Not long after my father's death, she tells my brother to get rid of everything. She doesn't keep a single memento. Not a cuff link or a golf tee or one of his handmade silk ties. It is all given to the homeless or put in the trash. My father wore toupees, which he kept on a wig stand. Someone had painted a resemblance of my father on it. It was the one thing of his that I wanted, but my brother tells me he threw that in the trash as well. "I felt kind of strange about it," my brother later admits. "Putting Dad's head in the trash."

None of this, of course, should have surprised me. I'd known for years that there was something wrong with my mother. Something off about her inability to feel for others especially when it came to grief. I was told of the deaths of beloved aunts and uncles in the car on the way to school. When it was time for my dog Cupcake to be put down, my mother called a cab. She gave the driver ten dollars to cart the dog to the vet, patted her on the head one last time, and shut the car door. While the housekeeper and I sobbed in the driveway, Cupcake scrambled against the glass as she was taken away.

I was young and didn't have a word for it, but I understood that my mother wasn't right. She was missing some component in her DNA. Over the years I learned to keep my sadness and grief to myself. My illnesses and injuries as well. I'd just assumed for whatever reason that I would see some tears over the man she'd been married to for sixty years. After all, she'd cried in front of the TV over JFK.

When it comes time to tell her about my broken ankle, I don't want to go into the details with her. By that time half of her is demented and the other half doesn't really care. I had learned long ago not to share my mishaps with my mother. She always has something worse going on. I resist telling her at all.

Now when she asks, "When will I see you?," I am able to answer, honestly, not for a while. And not feel guilty about it. But I do break down and call her to tell her I had an accident.

She replies, "Oh, I'm sorry to hear that. So, what else is new?"

64

Brooklyn, 2008

WE HIRE a dog walker. We've never needed one before. Someone is usually home to take Snowball, our fluffy white dog, out. But now we do. Somehow we find Eddie. Eddie comes by once a day. He's retired from a moving van company and is a veteran of Korea. Eddie has no teeth and can barely make it up my stairs. I have no idea how he walks dogs, but he does. Not many, but he has a few. He recites their names to me when he arrives as if they are his references that we should call. Homer is the only one I remember. Homer. Author of *The Odyssey*. How can I forget Homer and his journey of twenty years? Though for now I am Penelope, stuck at home but not yet weaving.

Eddie arrives every afternoon at about two o'clock to take poor Snowball out as he teeters through his final years. Eddie drags himself up the stairs, looking for the dog that is usually in my office at my feet. There is no escaping Eddie. He huffs and puffs his way into my office. I am literally his captive. He tells me about all the dogs he's ever owned or walked or fed a treat to. He talks about the war. On bad days (for me, that is) he speaks endlessly about all the furniture he's moved over the years. He's lived on our street since the year I was born and has innumerable tedious stories to share. The worst time is when he returns from the walk because then he has nothing but time on his hands.

One day he comes in and starts telling me about his rottweiler named Pete. Eddie returned home from work and found poor Pete dead on the floor. He was just three years old. When he took Pete to the vet, the vet couldn't figure out why Pete, a perfectly healthy dog, should have dropped dead. So the vet did an autopsy and found that Pete had swallowed a live wasp. The wasp had stung Pete to death inside of his gut. "And you know what," Eddie told me, "when they opened up Pete's stomach, that wasp was still alive. I saw it myself. It flew around the room and then it died."

65

EVERY NIGHT when I'm a girl I walk my dogs. There are two of them, the mother named Cupcake and the daughter Puppets, whom I helped whelp one night when Mars burned red in the sky and looked as if it was going to kiss the earth. They don't require leashes. They follow me wherever I go. I walk them down the long, dark suburban streets where we live. I walk them in the summer when the air is redolent with the smell of lilac and fresh-cut grass and in the winter when the streets are icy and the drifts piled high. My dogs always come when I call or whistle and I can walk them for hours. I walk them only in part because they need me to. Mainly I walk them so that I can get out of the house.

I have to escape my father's outbursts. This man who

plays jazz piano, cries at movies, and cannot listen to classical music without conducting can't seem to contain his free-floating rage either. The way the air turns heavy before a tropical storm, these outbursts are usually preceded by lectures. There is a right way and a wrong way for most things, including eating soup. With hot soup you push the spoon away from you, wiping the bottom on the side of your bowl as you blow onto it, thus avoiding dripping soup and a burned tongue. Cold soup you eat the opposite way, bringing the spoon toward you, wiping it on the edge. Or is it the other way around? I am never sure. There is a right way to load a dishwasher and a wrong way. A right way to dress and act. The slightest movements we make are scrutinized. There's a look in my father's eyes when he's getting angry. It's something out of fairy tales and admonishing children's books. These are the eyes of dragons and wild beasts. To this day I think they turned red.

Yet he's unpredictable. He might get angry if the lights were left on. Or he might not. If the garage door is open. We, his children, can't seem to figure out the rules, and all of these are reasons for lectures that lead to the minefield that becomes my childhood. Yet he never gets mad at the serious things—the big mistakes we might make. Once, shortly after I get my driver's license, I smash into the car of a friend of his that is parked in our driveway. I drive right into it. And all my father says is "Accidents happen. Be more careful next time." And once when our neighbor's daughter got pregnant and her father threw her out,

I overheard my father say, "If anything ever happened to Mary, she could always come home." Years later, when I am single and pregnant with my daughter, Kate, I will learn that he meant it.

Yet small things drive him crazy. The things that he somehow takes as personal slights. A sign that we disrespect him. And once the lecture begins, the fight can't be far behind. I sigh when being told to take a smaller bite of steak and he launches into "Get in the habit of being a lady." Then our mother will say, "Can't we have a meal in peace," and the next thing we know the shouting begins. My mother retreats to the kitchen, my brother to the TV. And I leave the house. I have the excuse of my dogs.

Fight or flight. I've always been interested in this primitive response. When I learned about it in school, it felt right. The two ways to deal with conflict. You face it or you flee it. It is, I suppose, if I wanted to analyze it (and I'm not sure I do), an explanation for my wanderlust. I am always in flight. It is a strange truth about me. I've never courted danger. That hasn't been my M.O. I was never into suicide by adventure. No, for me it was always about escape. It was always about getting away.

66

IF THEY COMMUNICATE AT ALL, tigers do so through a rare sound called chuffing. It resembles a deep, guttural purr. It is the sound they make when they greet each other in a nonthreatening way. It is also the sound they make when they are in a good mood. In the wild, tigers chuff when they meet on neutral territory. However, in captivity tigers often chuff when they see their keepers. A roar on the other hand means something else. It is a warning to other tigers to stay away. It may be used during mating or after a kill, but never during an attack. During an attack the tiger is silent.

67

India, 2011

IN THE BEIGE FLOWING GRASSES of the savanna it is almost impossible to detect the tiger's stripes. Still we look. I pan the grasslands with my binoculars. But if she is out there, we don't see her. For a long time we are silent and the only sounds are birds and the wind. Somewhere in the distance we hear the chatter of monkeys. But that is all. I don't know how long we are sitting when another jeep comes clattering up behind us. They've heard a call. For a few moments the drivers chat. There is the nodding of heads. In the other jeep a family sits, blankets over their heads. The kids have earphones on and look utterly bored. The parents don't seem very happy either. In fact, none of them smiles or even nods hello to me.

A few minutes later their jeep pushes on. Ajay and Sudhir look at me. "So?" I ask. Sudhir wants to persevere. And so does Ajay. And so do I. As the other jeep leaves us in a trail of dust, we pause, deciding what to do. Ajay and Sudhir talk in Hindi, and then take a road where we haven't been.

Our jeep bounces up and down the furrowed road as I clasp the frame. After a few hairpin turns we leave the dirt road and drive along a path that has been cut through thick brush. It is clear that no one comes here very often. After a few hundred yards the brush opens, and we enter a sunny meadow. For the first time in days I feel the sun beating down, warming me. The meadow sits on the shores of a wide pale-blue lake, surrounded by savanna and reeds. On the slopes around the lake, herds of spotted deer, sambar deer, antelope, and wild boar graze. Monkeys skitter across the paths and through the trees. Dozens of aquatic birds stand poised in the reeds, searching for fish.

We sit in silence for several minutes. Then Ajay says, "There is no tiger here." It is rhetorical. Of course, there is no tiger here. No scene would be so peaceful if a tiger were near. It is beginning to occur to me that I might not see a tiger in the wild. No matter how determined my driver and guide are, I think that it won't happen. Not now. Maybe never.

Still, in that warm circle of sun I find myself growing stronger. For the first time since I arrived, it seems I am not hacking away. It is as if I have suddenly been healed. More than anything I want to get out and walk. Clearly it is safe. Even I know that. I want to stretch my legs and walk around this turquoise-blue lake. I've grown stiff after days on airplanes and cars and now in this jeep, but it isn't just about that. I want to walk. Desperately. Though I have lost track of the days and the dates, I know that it is almost three years since my accident. I recall the truck driver I met at the hospital. Soon I will be beyond the point of improving. This is probably as good as it will get. And now, perhaps for the first time since my accident, I want to get up and walk and walk. Which is exactly what I cannot do. But it is as if I can't sit still. I can't contain myself. On the off chance that they will let me, I have to ask.

"Could I . . . go for a walk?"

They look at each other, then at me, incredulous. Then they laugh. "No," Ajay says, "you can't go for a walk."

"But there's no tiger here." They look at me again, and then politely say no. I nod. It is what I expected.

None of us speaks for a little while. Then Sudhir breaks the silence. "Almost nobody comes here," he says.

This surprises me. It is such a beautiful, tranquil place. "So why did you bring me?"

"Because you want to see."

I shrug. "Doesn't everyone?"

Both men shake their heads. "Most people only want to see tigers," Sudhir explains. "You want to see everything."

Again we sit in silence for a long moment. None of us wants to move. A flock of cormorants and egrets takes to the air and it fills with the flapping of their wings. "Shall we go?" Sudhir asks.

It is close to time to leave. And it is also time for me to say goodbye to my friends. Our time together is drawing to an end, and, as we all know, I haven't seen my tiger. "Just five more minutes," I say—a phrase I'm starting to imagine engraved on my tombstone—and the men agree. I don't want to leave. And neither do they. Together we sit, listening. But the jungle is surprisingly still. Sudhir is slow to turn on the engine. I am content to be here, but I can tell they are disappointed. The tiger has eluded us. "It takes patience, doesn't it, to find a tiger?" I ask, and they nod.

"And luck," Ajay replies.

68

CENTURIES AGO William Blake wrote the lines for which he is renowned. "Tyger, tyger, burning bright, / In the forests of the night; / What immortal hand or eye, / Could frame thy fearful symmetry?" It is difficult not to believe in a higher power when you gaze at this creature. Its black stripes appear painted on with the sure strokes of a calligrapher's pen. Or the work of a steady-handed tattoo artist. If you shave a tiger bald, its stripes will still appear on its skin.

69

IN 1972 I'm a graduate student at Harvard and my life is in shambles. I have no money, my boyfriend moves out when I'm at school, and two days later my bicycle is stolen. I'm struggling through *The Divine Comedy* in a graduate seminar I'm taking. On a hot July afternoon, I am reading *Purgatorio*. I already want to be a writer, but I have no idea where to begin or how to go about it. Then I fall asleep and have this dream.

I dream that I'm walking down a street in Paris and pass a café. Inside I see Gertrude Stein, Ernest Hemingway, and F. Scott Fitzgerald drinking Campari and soda. The café has its name written above the doorway. It is: Lasciate Ogni Speranza, Voi Ch'entrate—Abandon All Hope, Ye Who Enter Café. Strange name, I think, but I know that if I want to be a writer I have to go inside. So I do. I sit at a bistro table and order my own Campari and soda, and as I do my chair falls into a deep, dark hole in the center of the earth. I am inside what was called in medieval times an oubliette. A place where you are forgotten.

The darkness that surrounds me is absolute and as far as I can tell there is no way out. Suddenly six men appear, and they are carrying a coffin. They place it in front of me and leave and I understand that the only way out of this hole rests inside that coffin and it is my task to open it. So I do. And the coffin turns into a rolltop desk and paper for eternity.

A few weeks later I pack up my apartment in Cambridge and move to New York.

70

Brooklyn, 2008

THREE MONTHS into my ordeal Dr. Patel tells me I can walk. He's staring at my X-ray when he informs me. "The bone has healed." He looks clearly pleased. "You're good to go," he says. "Get some comfortable shoes. You should be fine." Buoyed, I actually thought I might be walking home from his office that day. I've brought some shoes with me. They're white sneakers that look like nurse's shoes. (I will subsequently abandon them outside a geriatric residence where they will be scooped up right away.) But they are the most comfortable shoes I have. I put them on, ready to set out.

And I can hardly take a step. The pain is unbearable. I try to hobble down the block toward home, but even with a cane I can't put any weight on my foot. Every step is excruciating. After half a block I have to stop and call a car service to take me home. Later a friend watches me, shaking her head as I clutch the banister, leaving her house.

I begin spending a lot of time online, studying the anatomy of the ankle. I come to understand why magnificent racehorses, such as Ruffian or Barbaro, are put down with a broken ankle. The racehorse rests all his weight on three tiny bones—the sesamoids. The human body is more or less the same. The ankle is perhaps the most complex of all the human joints. Shoulder, hip, knee replacements can all be done with fairly consistent results, but there is no successful ankle replacement as yet.

And I can't make it to the corner store for a quart of milk.

A week later I go to see Dr. Patel again. This time I don't care how I look. I don't bother to put on lipstick. I no longer want him to come to dinner or be my friend. My Stockholm syndrome relationship with him has come to an end. I just want to walk. I want him to tell me when I'll be better. He has betrayed me. Getting good shoes and walking is absurd. I've made no progress. My ankle swells hideously when I put any pressure on it at all. He's spoken to me about the possibility down the road of having the hardware in my ankle removed, but that's still a year away and I don't want another surgery.

For the first time I'm truly annoyed with him. Furious, in fact. I thought I'd be cured. It hasn't really occurred to me, though it will more and more, that some things are forever. And there's no miracle. I'm not sure why I was so naive, but I still believed that doctors made you well. I assumed that if you got hurt, they'd make you as good as new. I never wanted to think that something permanent can happen. That you can be forever changed.

Of course, I understood that death was real and illnesses

could be terminal. I knew there were things that nobody could do anything about. But it hadn't really sunk in that you might not be the same way you were. You might not be cobbled back together again. Suddenly I grasped that silly childhood rhyme. "Humpty Dumpty sat on a wall, Humpty Dumpty had a great fall. And all the king's horses and all the king's men couldn't put Humpty together again." I always thought it was nonsense about an egg. But it isn't nonsense; it's true.

In his office there is the usual two-hour wait, but this time I mind it. This time I'm annoyed. I keep asking the secretary how long it would be. "He had an emergency this morning," she tells me. Of course, a trauma surgeon has many emergencies. I know there are people much worse off than me. I think about that man I met in occupational therapy who'd had his bones crushed in a trucking accident. What he'd been through was a million times worse than anything that had happened me. I try to feel lucky, but I don't. I don't feel lucky at all.

I sit, staring at the TV. A game show is on. A woman is poised to win a car and she's jumping up and down, terrified that she'll get the answer wrong. She gets it wrong and loses the car, then breaks down in tears. At last I'm called. Dr. Patel is staring at my X-rays with his back to me. I sit in a straight-back leather chair while he leans back in his chair, his white shirt spotless, ironed. Who irons them? I wonder. "It still hurts," I tell him, and he nods. "It hurts a lot."

This is nothing new. He gives me a timeline—one I've heard before. In occupational therapy, physical therapy, and from him. In the first year I'll show the most improvement. In the second a little more, and by the third year . . . "Well"—he raises his eyes—"that'll be about the best you can do."

I wonder how much more progress I can make in this first year. Months into this ordeal and I can barely take a step. He outlines various options. "Now, I doubt that you'll need this, but you could get an ankle replacement down the road, though they really aren't very good yet. Hips, knees, those you can replace. But the ankle. You know it's the most complicated joint in the body. Few people give it much credit. I'd rather break any other bone . . ." He pauses here, realizing this might not be the best tack to take. "There's ankle fusion."

I blink. "What's that?"

It's as bad as it sounds. A steel rod is rammed up the heel into the tibia. The foot is secured in place, but you have no dorsal flexion. In other words, a permanent limp on a foot that would have no give. "You could still consider a second surgery to take the hardware out. That might improve your flexion. We could do that maybe next January at the earliest. That might help."

Another surgery, a rod rammed up my foot, an ankle replacement. None of these options makes me feel any better. "I just want to know . . ." My throat is catching, but I struggle to go on. "When will I be normal again?" I ask, tears welling.

He seems surprised by my question. As if no one has ever asked him such a thing before. "What do you mean by normal?" He has a perplexed look on his thoughtful face.

"You know . . ." My skin bristles. I can barely hold back my tears. "When will I be able to do things I used to? Like go to the store, take a walk in the park."

"I'm not sure you will . . ." He hesitates. "Quite frankly, I didn't know if you'd ever walk again." Never walk again?

"What do you mean?"

Dr. Patel gives me his most professional look, one I have rarely seen. It must be what he uses when he is delivering bad news. "I didn't know if your bone would heal. It was completely shattered."

I ask why he is telling me this months after my accident, and he replies quite succinctly that it was better for me not to know until now.

That night I can't sleep. Even my cocktail of drugs doesn't work. My doctor's words reverberate in my brain. "I didn't know if you'd ever walk again." How can such a thing be possible? And how would I live if it were so? In some way this is my own doing. Somehow this is my fault. My hubris, my need to prove myself. My accident. Mine alone. Meanwhile Larry sleeps soundly. He's exhausted. Between his job, his life, and caring for me, he has no time to himself. All he does is run around, then collapse at the end of the day.

I don't want to disturb him, but I'm up, my mind churning. The truth of this weighs on me like a ton of bricks. No matter what I do, it is possible that a part of me will never be the same. Humpty Dumpty. It's a lesson we all learn sooner or later. But I had to learn it in one fell swoop.

71

A SINGLE MALE TIGER requires a hundred square kilometers for its own private range. With poachers and population growth, that terrain is shrinking. So while there is no danger of extinction, as thousands exist in captivity, it is conceivable that the tiger will cease to exist in the wild.

The government of India's Project Tiger began in 1973 in an effort to preserve the Bengal tiger in the wild. It was started after a census showed that India's tiger population wasn't more than 1,800 (and it would continue to drop for a few years, due mostly to poaching). Its mandate was to create tiger reserves, and by 2008, there were more than forty Project Tiger reserves in India, covering 37,761 kilometers.

Project Tiger helped increase the tiger population to almost 3,500 in the 1990s. But a census in 2008 revealed that the population had once more dwindled to only 1,411. Since that census the government has pledged an additional $153 million to expand the project, setting up a Tiger Protection Force to combat poachers, and also a fund for the relocation of almost 200,000 villagers. The goal is to create a larger buffer zone so that tigers can move freely and, as you can imagine, minimize tiger/human interaction.

To date forty-eight areas have been declared tiger reserves. Some are relatively small, fewer than fifty square miles, but with large buffer zones that enable the tiger, especially the young males, to travel to other areas where villagers no longer live. Indeed, many villages have been moved away from the reserves. This has often led to conflict between the villagers and the conservationists. But about two decades ago the government came to see the value in preserving tigers.

The official number of tigers in India as of 2014 was about 2,226. The struggle remains to enable two apex predators (tigers and humans) to live in something that resembles harmony. Poachers remain the biggest problem. And the Chinese, who believe there is some secret to potency and longevity in the bones and the blood of the tiger, are the worst perpetrators.

To the Chinese the tiger is king, and they want to consume its marrow. In fact, the Chinese symbol for emperor is identical to the blaze that is found on every tiger's forehead. A vertical line with two horizontal lines through it. Indeed, it is possible that the Chinese character for king derived from the tiger's blaze. Though the individual tiger's stripes are unique, this blaze is always the same.

72

India, 2011

IN THE LATE AFTERNOON back at my bungalow I drag a blanket outside and lie in a circle of sun on the patio. The heat of the day warms me—just as the night chills me. The warmth soothes my head and my chest, and I imagine that I am getting well. Butterflies flit from hibiscus to bougain-villea. I am content in this patch of sun. The jungle is just beyond with its alarm calls, but no tigers. Where are the tigers? What if I don't see a tiger? After coming this far. How could I possibly not see one? If Ajay is the best guide in India and he can't find one, then how could I hope to? How disappointed will I be? What if I fail? And in this kind of quest can there be such a thing as failure?

I don't know. I'm not sure. Still lying there in the warmth, I experienced something that I've felt only a few times in my life. Crossing the Strait of Gibraltar, or gazing at the Black Sea. On a train traversing Siberia. In the water with dolphins swimming around me. In a man's arms. Nursing my daughter at my breast. It is the feeling that I want to stay here forever. I never want to leave. I want to hold on to this moment and never let it go. I want time to stop.

But that's the thing about travel. The point isn't to stay in one place. It is to move on. It is about seizing the moment, the hour, the day, with the understanding that it isn't forever. We have to move on. In the Sicilian language there is no future tense. You don't say, "I'll go to the beach tomorrow." You say, "I go to the beach tomorrow." The Sicilians understand the importance of staying in the present. It is what the traveler must learn as well.

All these thoughts jumble in my brain as I lie like a lizard, warming myself. I am in the middle of India in a place that my internist considered with dismay. The heat enters my bones and I believe, incorrectly, that it will heal me just as the fresh air of spring once helped heal my broken ankle. But more than anything it seems as if I have traveled halfway around the world just so I could sit alone in a warm circle of light on a patio in a jungle where wild beasts roam.

That night a fire burns in the fire pit in the center of the encampment. Two men sit near the fire and I come and sit not far from them. One is a very old man who is scantily clad and keeps a walking stick at his side. He nods at me as he hums softly to himself. The other I recognize as a worker at the hotel. I know we have no common language, yet we sit together, eyes on the flames. My face and hands are hot. My back is cold. Still, the fire feels good and I am happy for the company—even in the silence. I stay for a while, until the flames subside, and then head back to my bungalow.

Once again I am cold and tired, so I crawl into bed. I've left the windows open. There's no point in closing them. It's just as cold inside as out. I think I'll drift off to sleep but instead I lie there. I listen to the jungle sounds. A strange, guttural chatter, the calls of birds, a monkey's shriek in the night.

73

ONE MORNING outside of Atlanta, Georgia, a woman is making coffee. She has just let her dachshund out into the yard. The dog's name is Journey. The woman is pausing at the sink, thinking about her day. The sun is just rising as she pours her coffee. She's holding it, steaming in her hands, when a Bengal tiger jumps over her fence and pounces on her dog. The woman goes crazy, screaming. She's dialing 911 when suddenly two police officers, who had received reports of a tiger prowling in the suburbs of Atlanta, appear. One of the officers perches on top of the fence and shoots the tiger dead.

The tiger was a six-year-old circus star named Suzy. She belonged to a circus performer, Alexander Lacey, and was being transported along with thirteen other cats from Florida to Tennessee, where they were to live in a sanctuary. Suzy along with all the other cats had been retired from the Barnum & Bailey Circus. The truck had stopped outside of Atlanta for the night. No one knows how Suzy left the convoy nor did they notice her missing until they arrived at their destination and did a head count. They found that they had thirteen cats, not fourteen.

Journey survived.

74

REAL TRAVELERS, like real writers, move through the world like a child. With a child's sense of wonder and surprise. To move as if you've never been somewhere before, even if you've been there a thousand times. As if you are experiencing something for the first time. This is what my husband often says about me, and not always in a complimentary way. Every village we travel through, every painting we see, every meal eaten. It is as if I've not experienced any of this before.

Somewhere Proust writes that travel isn't about seeing new places. It's about seeing with fresh eyes. That is the thing about travel for me. I walk into a room as if I've never walked into one before. I meet a person as if I'm seeing him for the first time. Recently I read the strange case of a man who could not form memories. While I wouldn't envy this man, I do think it is an intriguing notion to wake up each day afresh.

It must be this sense of wonder that makes for good writers and good travelers. One summer we were in Basque Country in a little fishing village, and all day long boats floated past our living-room window. Every time a boat went by, I shouted to my husband, "Look, a boat." It didn't matter how many times a boat went by; each time I was enthralled.

75

LATE AT NIGHT I sneak downstairs. Groggy with sleep, I tiptoe to the landing on the basement stairs so I can watch my mother sewing. I watch her as if I am watching a TV show—never taking my eyes off the screen. She's hunched over a quilting frame that takes up much of our basement. Under the light of a single bulb she's making the tiniest of stitches. Almost everything she does is by hand. There will be tens of thousands of stitches before she's done. She's making the bedspreads, pillow shams, and curtains for my room.

From the stairs I can see only the back of her head and the smoke from her cigarette, which rises like a signal to warn the tribe. She never knows I'm there. Never hears me or sees me, and I don't dare disturb her. If I do, she'll send me back to bed. She works into the night. My mother began quilting when we moved into the house I grew up in. I was three years old. She'll finish when I enter middle school. This task will occupy most of my childhood. When I leave for college and my parents move into the city, she throws the quilts away.

My mother was a gifted seamstress. She had a certificate in fashion from the Art Institute of Chicago. She had dreams of being a designer. For years she made every dress she wore. She married late—in her mid-thirties—when her own mother had given up all hope for her youngest daughter. Once she married my father, she mainly sewed Halloween costumes for her children. In my life I have been a brontosaurus, a swashbuckler, and a money tree. No princess, no fairy queen for me. I didn't even get to be a witch. She decided what creatures I would be, what clothes I would wear to school.

The night I was a money tree, boys at a school party ripped off my paper bills. I walked home crying, the wind blowing through my naked branches. One afternoon our puppy teethed on the arm of an expensive chair and my mother sat on the floor, reupholstering it. She finished just as my father walked in the door. He never noticed. My mother wanted to travel. She wanted to see the world. Instead she spent six years quilting my bedspreads.

I want to distract her. I want her to come upstairs and tell me a story, but she rarely does. She's too impatient to sit with me for very long. She has patience only for her quilting. "These are for you," she tells me, even as they occupy all of her time. But they are beautiful. Pink and white with a soft cottony feel, the way I imagine my mother's skin must be. In the years I sleep in my room, they will smell of smoke and of her perfume, Replique.

It is my father who tucks me in. He sits at the side of my bed, making up stories about a homesick snowflake that tumbles to earth, about a brook and a nasty bridge. He sings me the Whiffenpoof song about the poor little lambs who've gone astray until I drift to sleep. Not my mother. She stands in my doorway, a silhouette against the doorframe, blowing me a kiss. "Did you catch it?" she asks, and I always say I did.

76

India, 2011

IT IS DISHEARTENING, leaving Pench. After all these days of tiger safari, the only pugmarks I've managed to see are on the monogrammed towels in my room. And I know how disappointed Ajay and Sudhir are that we didn't find my tiger. Later on Facebook they will e-mail me pictures of all the tigers they have seen since my departure. "You have to come back, Mary," Ajay will write. How have they seen all these tigers and I didn't manage to see one?

Though we have not communicated in days, Dinesh, my driver, shows up as planned. He looks well and rested, his shirt white and pressed. I have no idea where he has been for the days I've been here. I am late getting ready and he is a little anxious. We are leaving Pench later than Dinesh would have liked. It is true; I am a dawdler and he is very punctual. But I don't want to leave. I wanted to find my tiger with Ajay and Sudhir, but that wasn't to be.

As we start off, he sees that I am still coughing. In fact, my cough has returned with a vengeance. "You aren't any better?" he asks.

"No," I tell him. "I think I am worse."

Heading due east, we pass the Tiger Woods Resort and at first I think it's named after the fallen-from-grace golfer, but instead it means quite literally what it says. These are the woods where tigers technically roam. Though none

This is the journal I took with me to India. I wrote and drew in it every day.

This is some of the first wildlife I saw when we approached Pench Tiger Reserve. It was so beautiful to see mother and baby together.

These white-spotted deer are at the alert. Perhaps the sambar deer have warned them that a tiger is near.

This young wild boar suddenly came out of the jungle, took one look at us, then quickly ran back again.

Ajay, Sudhir, and I are pausing just after lunch. But as you can see from his expression, Ajay is always listening.

Sudhir is trying to figure out how to put his snake back in the bag.

Ajay and Sudhir brought me to this peaceful place because I wanted to see everything.

Every day this mahout and his elephant face the dangers of the jungle.

This was my first sign that a tiger was near. At Kahna.

I rode my elephant into the bush and saw this tiger resting.

She leapt onto the road and stood there.

She is turning, just as she is ready to go and head back into the jungle. I spent a long time watching her leave.

that have crossed paths with me. Clearly this isn't the best season for seeing tigers. Still, I am sorry to leave it behind and sad to say goodbye to Ajay and Sudhir.

I start coughing again. "You need more cough drops and whiskey," he tells me. It is not a question but a statement, and I agree. Especially about the whiskey. I think I need a doctor as well, one who can prescribe antibiotics, but I have no idea where or when that will happen.

We pass a pair of bullocks with their horns painted bright blue. An old man totters by on a bicycle with an enormous sack of rice on his head. It is about four in the afternoon on the national highway, and we hit rush hour. The two-lane road is burgeoning not only with cars and trucks but also with oxen. When the oxen's day's work is done, the farmers let them loose from the fields. Each ox knows his way home and they just saunter along.

Dinesh honks his horn endlessly as he weaves his way around every car, motorbike, truck, taxi, child on a bike, and beast of burden. Vehicles rush toward us, head-on, while we careen in and out of whatever traffic is before us. It is like a video game that's real. Pedestrians amble along as well. Women in saris of saffron, emerald, and salmon walk behind hay trucks, tending the load. Two friends meet on opposite sides of the road and decide to have a chat. So they just step into the middle of the road and stand there, talking. They aren't fazed by the innumerable vehicles that veer around them, beeping, and shouting drivers, as they catch up on how the family's doing.

One of the excellent things about Dinesh—beyond the water bottle and towelettes that he provides—is that he is very knowledgeable about the bathrooms en route. He knows how long it will be between one good bathroom and the next. And he knows which ones are, relatively speaking, clean. With this in mind we make a preemptive pit stop, then push on to Kahna, which is about a four- or five-hour drive. At Seoni we pull over in front of a convenience store amid a deluge of scooters, rickshaws, pickup trucks.

On the median strip a herd of feral white pigs with piglets grazes. Sacred cows promenade through the middle of the business district. I use the facilities as Dinesh gets me more cough drops and whiskey, of which I take a hearty swig. Back on the highway a snowy egret smashes into our windshield, bounces into the middle of the road, then flies away, apparently unscathed.

It is dusk when we leave the main road. We are now traveling on the outskirts of the game reserve. In the gullies children are rushing home. Boys play in the middle of the road. We pass huts made of wooden slats that sell soft drinks, milk, aspirin. Basic supplies. We are in the buffer zone. But as I see the children on bikes dashing around, I can't help but wonder: Aren't they afraid? Isn't there some risk, well, of being eaten?

Dinesh tells me we have perhaps another half hour on this road, which grows bumpier and bumpier by the minute. Trucks barrel toward us. I finally share with him that

I'm disappointed that Ajay and Sudhir didn't find a tiger. "Oh, you will see a tiger," Dinesh says. "We are coming to a dry riverbed and in the years I've been coming here, I've seen at least sixteen tigers at this one spot. I know you'll see a tiger. I'm ninety percent sure that you will." But as we come to the riverbed there are no tigers to be seen.

It is pitch-black as we drive through a village to Chitvan Jungle Lodge. We pass a kind of pension. I can see open rooms with bunk beds and Dinesh tells me that is where he'll be staying while I am at the hotel. This hadn't occurred to me. I hadn't thought, really, about where Dinesh would stay, and it makes me sad to think of him in his proper white shirt sleeping in a bunk bed.

At last we pull into the property of the hotel. Just as Pench was lush and rustic, Kahna is open, with large vegetable gardens, a huge expanse of lawn. It is more like where I imagined the British would stay during the Raj, and I'm not far from wrong. As I check in, I explain that I'm not feeling well, and I would love some soup and tea. The clerk nods and leads me through a garden of winding paths, past a large vegetable patch. In the patch the leaves of banana and avocado trees are crumpled and brown. "It has never been this cold," the clerk tells me.

As we walk toward my room, I can see my breath. The chill enters my lungs, and I start to cough. "I'm sorry," I explain. "I'm a little sick." My room is a large one-bedroom suite and no sooner am I inside than a tray with my dinner arrives. The man who brings it bows, then walks away without showing me his back. On the tray along with chapatis and curry, I find bread and butter and a strange, oily chicken soup. Another small tray with a pot of tea is delivered.

There are space heaters in the rooms, which almost make me cry, but the rooms are so spacious, they barely make a dent in the cold. Still I turn them all on, then get into bed to read. No one can see me, so I don't draw the curtains. Outside, a Cheshire Cat smile of a moon grins. The night is filled with jungle sounds, but nowhere, for me at least, does the tiger roar.

77

IN ORDER for a tiger to make a kill, she must sneak up on her prey in a crouch. And then she must pounce and chase it down with all her speed. But she's a sprinter, not a long-distance runner. So she must rely on stealth. Once the tiger has made her kill, she will hold on to it until her heartbeat slows.

78

THE TAHITIANS don't have a word that means "art." The closest expression in their language translates to something like "I'm doing the best I can." Ever since I heard this it has become a kind of mantra to me. I try and apply it to my own work, to my students and anyone who shares his or her work with me. If we live with the idea of perfection, we will never do anything. The notion paralyzes us, but doing the best we can, this is possible. I recall a friend many years ago who said he wanted to write like William Faulkner. I told him I just wanted to write a good scene every day or so. My friend ceased writing long ago, but it appears that I am still plodding along.

I am reminded of that moment in *The Fugitive Kind* when a woman shows Marlon Brando a bad landscape painting she has done. He looks at it and, in his Marlon Brando way, says nothing. But the woman replies, "I know they aren't very good, but I feel better when I do them."

79

WHEN I'M A GIRL, my hair is long and lush. Strangers like to touch it when they walk by. Once when I'm standing in line at Leo's Delicatessen, waiting for a corned beef sandwich, a woman fondles my ponytail as if she plans to steal it. When I turn twelve, my mother tells me I need a trim. "You're old enough," she says, "to go on your own."

So I do. I make an appointment with the hairdresser and on a Saturday afternoon ride my bike there. The assistant washes and admires my beautiful, silken hair. Then I sit in the chair and the hairdresser asks me what I want. The pixie cut, as it is called, is popular then. Several of my friends have done this with their hair. "I want a pixie," I tell her.

She looks at me a little surprised. "Does your mother know?"

"She told me to get a haircut." So the woman chops off my long tresses. She gives me bangs, a shaggy top. She goes happily about her job and we both admire it when she's done.

I ride home, but my mother isn't there. There's a rock on the lawn at the end of our driveway and I'm sitting there like a lizard, warming in the sun, when she pulls in from the store. She rolls down her window. "Oh my god, what have you done?" She shakes her head in fury. "What have you done to your hair?"

My mother is my mirror. She tells me how I look, what to wear. This matters to her more than anything. If I look good, I get a thumbs-up. If I don't, she asks rhetorically, "Is that what you're going to wear?" Throughout my teens we fight, and it is mostly over my appearance. Not my grades or my friends and how I behave. How I look always matters much more than how I feel.

Every season she takes me to the mall. "You need some spring clothes," she'd say. Then she picks out what she wants me to wear. She rejects everything I seem to like. The blouse I love tugged at my breasts. She yanks on it to show me. The skirts I want are too long or too short. I always seem to need another size, a different cut. Jackets make me look boxy. Sweaters busty. I need clothes that minimize. With each outfit, I step out of the fitting room and wait for her to tell me what is wrong.

In the 1930s my mother was working at Saks on Michigan Avenue in Chicago, selling ladies underwear. But before she married, she designed and made all her own clothes. Her idol was Coco Chanel. One day an important designer came into Saks to show the saleswomen how to dress the mannequin. As he was trying to explain something that no one seemed able to grasp, my mother held up the sketch she'd just drawn. "Is this what you mean?" He asked her how she learned to do that. My mother shrugged. "I taught myself," she said.

The designer helped my mother get a scholarship to the Art Institute of Chicago, where she studied fashion until her father refused to give her the carfare she needed to get to school. But fashion was her thing. If she'd been born a little later, she might have had a fashion line of her own. Instead, I become her mannequin. Dressing me becomes her project.

I must subject myself not only to these shopping expeditions but also to the visits to the tailor. I dread these outings. Everything has to be shortened or lengthened, let in or let out. Shoulders need lifting. Seams have to be opened. As my breasts grow, special snaps are sewn into my blouses to keep them from "opening." I stand on raised platforms, scowling at myself in the mirror. The seamstress, her mouth full of pins, rotates me so that my mother can approve. But I have beautiful clothes. My closets are full of pleated skirts; cable-stitched sweaters filled my drawers. On the spare bed in my room clothing piles up. I never wear the same thing two days in a row. I never hang anything up. I never put anything away.

As I grow older, I develop a horror of large stores. Inside of Marshall Field's I can barely breathe. My mother has a habit of wandering off, and I'm trying to find her. Once at the Harvard Coop my mother disappears in office supplies. As I race around, looking for her, I bump into two friends I haven't seen in a while. They ask me how I'm doing, and I reply I'm fine, but I've just lost my mother. They offer their condolences.

When I move to New York after college, I can't walk into Bloomingdale's or Saks without feeling as if my head will explode. I find a small shop in Manhattan run by two Korean sisters. They help me decide what I'll look good in. I hardly have to think about it at all. Black slacks, black dresses. Black as often as I can. On my own I buy shoes, bags, jewelry, scarves. I buy them from street vendors and at small craft fairs, from little boutiques. I am always looking for earrings, something to spiff up my hair. I buy things that can't be returned, that don't need to be altered. Years later a friend will comment that I accessorize well.

80

India, 2011

MY NEW GUIDE, Vibhav, is about as different from Ajay as anyone could be. He's bubbly, loquacious. His English is perfect, and he seems to be a man with a plan. He shows up, pretty much dressed for safari in khaki shorts and a khaki shirt, floppy hat. He holds a clipboard and has binoculars around his neck. Unlike Ajay, for whom I had to pay extra, Vibhav is the guide assigned to me during the entire time I'm in Kahna. He is bright and perky as I approach the jeep.

"Ready to go, Miss Morris," he says. I'm almost expecting him to salute but grateful that he doesn't. Our driver, Sonu, introduces himself. He speaks little English, but Vibhav explains he is also a good guide as well as a mahout. Sonu's father is a senior mahout. The role of mahout is handed down by fathers to their sons and begins when a boy is very young. He will receive a young elephant that will be his to train and care for during the duration of the elephant's life. We will probably run into Sonu's father on his elephant during the day.

We set off past fields of workers in the buffer zone. This is the land of the Baagh people, who worship the tiger as a god. They also worship the trees and the land. Men, stooped over, are pouring bladders of water down holes. They are catchers of rats and mice, which they will cart back to their villages to roast over flames. Rats and mice are a delicacy. On the side of the road on a large stone slab two girls pound stacks of bullock manure into patties that are drying in the sun. These will provide fuel for their fires and adobe for their houses.

We pause at the gate to Kahna to get our paperwork in order. Then the gate is lifted and we're inside. We drive down the dusty road with Vibhav chatting away. I miss Ajay's pensive reserve, but at the same time Vibhav explains a great deal to me. "If you ever meet a tiger in the jungle," Vibhav tells me, "don't run. Stand up very tall. He will not recognize you as prey. His prey come on four legs." I may not be prey, but at the same time I would be encroaching on his territory.

He may not want to eat me, but I have read an account in which a tiger grabbed a man who was tracking him by his backpack and shook him until he broke most of the bones in the man's body. While the chances of my meeting up with a tiger now are slim, since I am stuck in this jeep, I appreciate the advice. Vibhav gives me this final warning: "So if you run into a tiger on the road, don't crouch. Don't take your eyes off of him. And walk backward very slowly."

I'm having trouble envisioning this. I don't know many people who under the circumstances wouldn't run for their lives, let alone walk away backward. I'm impressed with those people who can roll into a ball and let a grizzly bear use them to play soccer. I'd like to believe I'd be the one to crumple to the ground in surrender. But I'm pretty sure I wouldn't. Once while swimming off the coast of Honduras I found myself being followed by a barracuda—the most feared animal in the Caribbean because it can snap and in an instant rip off a man's calf. I swam like a madwoman to shore.

"Last year," Vibhav goes on, "a mahout was killed by a tiger." Every morning the mahout must go into the jungle to find his elephant, which grazes freely at night. This mahout was out in the early morning, and he came between a tigress and her cubs. Despite his training not to run, he ran. He panicked. He had his walkie-talkie, so he called for help, but the tiger chased him to a tree, which the man climbed. Tigers can't really climb trees, but then the man fell from the tree and was devoured.

I make a face. "You mean . . . eaten?"

Vibhav nods somberly, as does Sonu, who seems to be following this story. His father, after all, is a mahout, as is Sonu. The dangers are real. "Okay, so I'll try not to run," I tell them and they both laugh.

"Yes," Vibhav says, "and never come between a tiger and her cubs."

81

"YOU WERE ONCE WILD HERE," Isadora Duncan said. "Don't let them tame you." As a dancer, of course she understood this. But as a mother, when her children drowned in the Seine, she did not go wild. She went nearly mad. She sought men who would impregnate her, young lovers who would provide new offspring to replace all that she had lost. When that failed, she formed a dance company of girls and referred to them as her children. Many took her last name. And then she died that famous, ludicrous death—her scarf getting caught in the wheel of a car and essentially decapitating her when she was flung from the vehicle. But even in the midst of her deepest suffering, Duncan understood that in her art she had to be wild. She was never meant to be tamed.

82

IN PICTURES from the journey I am like this. Grim-faced. Frowning at moments when I should be laughing. In front of the Trevi Fountain, the Eiffel Tower, Buckingham Palace, I look more as if I'm headed to the dentist than on the grand tour. Even in the pictures where I strike odd poses, mimicking the statues in the Villa Borghese gardens, there's no expression on my face. These could be the mug shots for crimes I have yet to commit. It is my mother who puts them into the album. I can't bear to look at them. Yet she's hardly smiling either. Her unhappiness seems to mirror mine.

It is 1962 and my mother scoops me up and takes me to

Europe with her. I am her reluctant traveling companion because my father refuses to go. What went on between my parents was never clear to me. I suspected things that I was too young to understand. When I was very young, their twin beds were pushed as far apart as they could go. I never cuddled between them, but instead bounced from bed to bed like a Ping-Pong ball. When I was about ten, I gave my mother a silky nightgown for her birthday, pink and transparent. I think I picked it out myself—only to have her walk into my room one night and hurl it at me. "I don't need this," she said in her fury. I don't remember when she moved into the maid's room, but I do remember that she never left.

And now my mother wants to flee. (An art I will perfect myself in the coming years.) And she intends for me to accompany her. But I am a sullen teenager in love with an Irish boy from across the tracks when my mother decides to drag me off to Europe. I know nothing of her scheme when she picks me up one day after school. "Get in the car," she tells me. "We're going to get your passport." I didn't want a passport, and I didn't know why I needed one. My summer would revolve around only three things: learning touch typing, spending afternoons at the beach, and being in the arms of the Irish boy. But my mother has other plans.

As we drive south on Edens Highway from the suburbs where we lived to downtown Chicago, she explains. She intends to take me to Paris, London, and Rome as soon as school lets out. It's clear that she isn't really asking. My mother rarely asks my opinion about anything concerning me. But that's beside the point. She wants to get away. She's never been anywhere really, except to Idaho one summer—a place she detested. And she's longing to travel. Anyone who knows my mother knows this. Now she wants to do the grand tour.

I'm appalled. "Can't you ask Dad?" I whine. We both know that my father will never go with her. He hates to go anywhere except to his office, the golf course, or his club. I am to be her reluctant companion, an accidental tourist for six weeks on the road. This is my worst nightmare. "I don't want to," I tell her, staring out as the flat Midwestern landscape speeds by.

My mother grips the wheel with her white gloves. "You're going," she says.

The passport office is located in a dreary green institutional-type building. Inside, my mother takes a number, gets some forms, and then sits down on one of the gray plastic chairs. As we wait, a woman in some kind of military uniform marches in. She's wearing high boots and a cap and begins to stomp around, then gives the Sieg Heil salute to me, clicking her heels together. I'm terrified, but my mother laughs. "It's awful, I know," she says, "but she's just crazy." Still this woman makes me feel that the world I am about to enter is a dangerous place and I'm its reluctant voyager.

A few weeks later an official envelope arrives which my mother hands to me with a flourish as if I am being anointed for something. But for what? Inside I find my passport with the gold seal of the United States on its cover. I flip through its virgin pages, then tuck it into the passport case my mother has given me with my initials inscribed on it. I don't give this passport much thought. Nor do I understand its secret powers until we arrive in Paris early on a Saturday morning, groggy from sleep, and the French customs official in his dark blue uniform and high red hat raises his stamp and imprints it on my passport. He hands it back to me and welcomes me to France. "*Bienvenu, mademoiselle.*" I have crossed my first border.

In Paris we stay in the Hotel de Vendôme. My mother admires its canopied mahogany beds, its red damask curtains. She savors peach melba in the evenings and washes her feet in the bidet.

Since I was very little, she'd wanted to go to Paris. She named our first dog Renoir. When I was in grammar school, she insisted that I learn French. (Before I graduated from high school my mother had seen to it that all the grammar schools in our town offered French by the sixth grade.) Every Tuesday afternoon I went over to see poor Monsieur LaTate, who had a nervous tic and seemed despondent as I struggled with the irregular verbs. I was pretty miserable too. But my mother was adamant. She was a Midwestern housewife who belonged more in a literary salon than in a supermarket. And now at last we've gotten out of the boonies. We're in France.

My mother quickly falls in love with Paris. During the day she dresses to perfection in her dark suit with black patent leather pumps, white gloves, and always her strand of cultured pearls. They are a rather cheap strand—something she often complains about—but she wears them everywhere as we clomp around Paris, where she searches for eyeliners and perfumes (Chanel No. 5; Replique, of which she buys boxes to take home), handbags and shoes. She doesn't care what anything costs. "So broke, so broke," she likes to say. We are at this time in our lives "comfortable." This isn't to last forever, but on this trip she doesn't bat an eye as she buys me a royal blue cloth coat to match my eyes ("Definitely your color"). She drags me to every Monet and monument she can find. We climb the steps of Sacré-Coeur and find a little bistro where, for the first time, I sip wine, then stagger back to the hotel. We dine on the Seine on a Bateaux Mouche with Paris illumined all around us. My mother doesn't just visit Paris. She drinks it in.

We push on to Rome, where we stay at the Flora. My mother is sure that Marcello Mastroianni passed us in the street. A handsome young doorman calls me Miss America and flirts with me in a way that I think my mother finds charming. "How is Miss America? Where is Miss America going today?" And we are going everywhere. For the first days, we hire a guide who takes us all over Rome. It seems as if my mother never wants to stop. When he mentions that he is taking us to the oldest market in the city, she asks what she can buy there. "I wouldn't know, madam," he replies in his accented English. "It's been closed for two thousand years."

My mother is enchanted with it all, even the street sign that reads "Senso Unico," which she thinks is the name of our street (which, in fact, is the Via Veneto). We have an audience with the pope—and five thousand other people—at the Vatican. The nuns shove to get past us. A priest from Chicago, Father Cozzio, who doesn't care that we're Jewish, leads us by the hand. For years afterward my mother will remember his name. One afternoon, we go across the street to the famous Eva of Rome, where we have our hair done. Mine is washed, set, and combed into a fluffy confection that is then sprayed. I hate it. My doorman gives me a wink. "Miss America, what have you done to your hair?" he asks as I walk by.

Back in our room, my mother lies down to take a nap and I stick my head in the sink, comb out my hair, and towel-dry it back to a semblance of its former self. Then I head out on my own. Leaving the hotel, I cross over to the Villa Borghese, happy to be alone, walking in the shade. But it is not long before I begin to hear sharp whistles, the sounds of men calling.

Some follow me shouting "*Bella*" and other things I don't understand. It takes me a few minutes to realize that these catcalls are for me. I am both frightened and flattered. I find myself being coaxed into this world of doormen and strange men, and my Irish boy back home suddenly pales. Though I don't know what they are saying, I understand that I'm on the brink of something and my life is about to change.

From Rome we take a bus to Florence and, as we leave Rome, the bus driver's wife hands him a lunch pail and takes away his bag of dirty clothes. When they kiss good-bye, he cradles her face in his hands in a loving way. "Italians are so romantic," my mother says. As we ride along, I gaze out at ruins and cypresses, vineyards and olive trees, until we stop in a small town for lunch. Here another woman greets our bus driver. She embraces him, kissing him on the lips, then hands him a parcel of clean clothes. As he goes to spend his lunch break with her, my mother laughs and laughs. "I don't get it," I say.

"Oh you will. One day you will."

Florence, Pisa, Genoa. We bus across Italy. We head on to Nice, but en route we stop for a night in the sea-side town of La Spezia. On a warm summer evening we dine on a balcony with the sea stretching before us. With the sun still shining, we eat delicious grilled fish and sip cold white wine. As she sits, looking out to sea, my mother fondles her strand of cultured pearls. She's worn them almost every day for years. As the waiter comes to clear, she unwinds the strand over her head. "I'm sick of these," she says. And, laughing, she hurls them into the sea.

83

India, 2011

THE NEXT MORNING when I open my door Vibhav is there to greet me. He stands in his khaki shorts and safari hat, clipboard in hand, beaming. "Are you ready, Miss Morris? Have you had your tea?" I nod, unable to hide my dismay. Though I spent only a few days with them, I miss Ajay and Sudhir. I want Ajay to be listening to the wings of birds and Sudhir trying to get a python back into a gunnysack. I miss having the best guide in India even if Vibhav is a very nice and, I'm sure, competent man.

I'm as ready as I suppose I'll ever be.

"Then let's go." After more than a week of searching for tigers, I have seen none. Yet Vibhav seems endlessly optimistic. Though I can't blame the messenger, I recall that troubled flicker that went across Catherine's face when I saw her back in Delhi. It is just too cold for tigers to be on the prowl. "So how did you sleep?" Vibhav asks as we make our way through the chilly morning air to the jeep. "Are you feeling better?" I nod again though I'm not feeling any better at all. "I think we will go in a different direction today. Tigers are very smart. They know the way the jeeps tend to go and so they head into another part of the jungle. We will try and outsmart them."

How can I tell him that all I want to do is stay under the covers? With a scarf around my neck and hot-water bottle in hand, I can barely talk for fear I'll start hacking. I think of the method of the servants of the maharaja who sewed white sheets together to flush the tiger out. Perhaps we should try this instead. But Vibhav, who knows I am sick, assures me. We will stay out for only a few hours. "I'll have you back by noon."

As we drive along, he points out things I have already seen. He tells me what I already know. Only once does he raise his hand as if he hears something. Then just before noon we turn around. He tells me sadly that today there aren't even alarm calls. "It's as if the jungle," he says, "is asleep."

84

EXCEPT FOR A BRIEF PERIOD of intense mating and raising her cubs, the tiger is always alone. Like the shark she moves forward. She never backtracks. Unless she has no other choice, a tiger will never retrace her steps. Rather she will move in a circle, eventually returning to where she began. Curiously there are no tigers in Africa. People often make this mistake. They could have easily crossed over from Asia, but for whatever reason they never did. No one knows why.

85

AN ACQUAINTANCE told me something that her grand-mother, a great traveler, told her. When you are young, you travel to far-flung places. When you are in your for-ties, you go to Europe. In your sixties, to Canada and Mex-ico. And when you are old, see America. I thought I was done with my far-flung places. I was hobbled. And I hadn't seen forty in a long time.

86

Paris, 2009

ABOUT A YEAR after my accident, we go to Paris to get away. I've been thinking about tigers for several months and I'm not sure I want to be thinking about them at all. For the moment I just want to be in Paris—a city I love. Years ago I lived in Paris with a mother and her son, Jean-Michel. Jean-Michel and I had lost track of each other over the years. Then about a decade ago we reconnected and since then I've tried to see him and his Algerian wife, Karima, often.

We have drinks with them one night. I tell Jean-Michel that I'm looking for a book (I no longer recall the title, but it had nothing to do with tigers), and he suggests that I try the bookstore at Place Saint Sulpice. "And while you are there, you should look in the church," he mentions as an afterthought. "There are two very good Delacroix frescoes." I am not a huge fan of churches and in all honesty I can't say that I'd ever given Delacroix much thought. But on a cold and rainy afternoon we stop in the church and there are two amazing frescoes, including one with an incredible angel and another of a terrified horse. We sit for a long time, gazing at them, before moving on. At the bookstore we find the book I want and head home.

The next day is Sunday, another rainy day. A friend had recommended the Museum of the Art and History of Judaism. He said that they have a very good exhibit on Moroccan Jews there and I am somewhat interested. We set off early and got to the museum. The museum is a little like getting into a fortress with all the security, but once inside I am somewhat surprised to see that the exhibit of Moroccan Jews begins with paintings and sketchbook entries by Delacroix. He had gone to North Africa in search of the exotic and found it in these Moroccan Jews. I spend a great deal of time with these paintings and sketches, making notes in my journal.

On Monday Larry and I get up early and go to a café, and after an hour or two I want to go to a store I know for some art supplies, so we head out. Except we go the wrong way. We are walking and walking and after a while I realize we are heading away from the store, but then I see the sign. To the Delacroix house. It is beginning to dawn on me that I cannot escape Delacroix. That somehow he is becoming important to me. I feel as if I am following an invisible map—nothing I can see or even of my own making, but it is a map nonetheless and now I must follow it wherever it might lead me.

We find the house and pay the admission. The ticket seller asks if we would also like to purchase a pass to the Louvre because most of the larger and more important Delacroixes would be seen there. I decline the offer. The last time I was in the Louvre I was still in a wheelchair and got trapped during a fire alarm in Grecian sculpture. It wasn't a good memory.

We walk into the house that includes Delacroix's atelier. He moved to this house late in life. The studio where he'd painted his most important works was demolished and he'd had to move. This was apparently heartbreaking for him, but he built this new studio though he did not live that long after moving in.

I wander through two rooms and then come to a third, and there I stop dead in my tracks. For not only did Delacroix paint Moroccan Jews in his search for the exotic but he also drew and painted tigers. Lots of tigers. The little room that I come to is full of them, with a note informing the viewer that the actual painting of the tigers is, of course, in the Louvre.

We return to the front desk and ask if it is too late to add the Louvre to our ticket. An hour later we are fighting the hordes, pushing our way through the busloads of tourists, until at last I come to stand in front of the beautiful Delacroix painting of two tigers. The creature that I am trying to avoid has hunted me down. As I stand before the enormous canvas, I feel as if I have been led here by design. As if despite whatever I told myself before I came to France, this was where I've been going all along.

87

Brooklyn, 2008

WHEN I STILL CAN'T WALK, I decide to get a second opinion. A former student of mine is an orthopedic surgeon in Minneapolis and I ask him, "Who is the best ankle person in New York?" He gives me a name, a surgeon he has worked with, and I look him up. Indeed, he is supposed to be one of the best in the world. I call for an appointment and snag one that is a few weeks away. They don't take insurance. And he is very expensive. But I want to know what he thinks.

The day of my appointment I'm optimistic. I bring my X-rays and Dr. Patel's report. And then I get to the office and I wait. I wait and wait and finally he is able to see me. Without as much as a hello or asking what happened he grabs the X-rays and puts them up on his light box. He looks at them, nodding. "This surgeon did a very good job on you. I couldn't have done any better myself."

I am relieved to hear this. After all, we trusted Dr. Patel on the basis of a handshake.

"But you'll need an ankle replacement in five years. You won't be able to walk on this foot much past that." I start to ask a question, and then I realize that for him our appointment is done. It has taken ten minutes and cost me five hundred dollars, and this is all he has to say.

I walk out into the city, feeling as if I've just been fired from my job. A job I never wanted in the first place. An ankle replacement in five years when this surgery barely exists. I decide I won't listen to that doctor. I will walk. To prove it I don't get on the subway. I walk for blocks, tears in my eyes, but I keep walking.

88

MY MOTHER never goes outside unless she has to. She doesn't like it. She doesn't like trees or lakes. She doesn't like a spring day or a cold winter night. I never see her taking in a deep breath or putting her hands into the soil. I don't think of her as being outdoors. Instead I see her in front of the vanity table that she keeps in my room. Here she sits for hours on end, preening, getting ready to be somewhere—a canasta game, a luncheon, a cocktail party. Some occasion that rarely includes me.

I'm never quite sure why her vanity is in my room and not theirs, but it is. It doesn't matter if I'm studying for an exam or taking a nap. I look up and see her there, dabbing bright red lipstick off with a tissue. The vanity includes a large mirror and all her makeup and perfumes and combs and hair spray. All her hand creams and face creams and makeup removers. It also contains my brushes and colognes and, eventually, makeup.

I watch her for hours, sitting in front of the mirror, applying her lipstick and rouge, the Replique she dabs behind her ears, on her wrists and the backs of her knees (don't ask me why). I see my mother in dresses of elegant wool or crepe, gowns, tailored suits. There are pictures of her in Idaho in shorts, and on my wall in Brooklyn I have an image of my mother as a girl in jodhpurs, a neatly tucked-in shirt, her flaming red hair parted down the middle. A cowgirl I never knew.

When I think of my mother, she is either elegantly dressed or wearing a nightgown. It seems as if for her there is no middle ground. I never see her wear any shoes besides high heels. Those stilettos whose clatter is the first thing my father heard after his ear surgery. But I love the outdoors. I love the lake, the woods. The long walks to school. My father is the same. He plays golf and tennis, and he walks everywhere.

But my mother lives her entire life inside. I never ride a bike with her or walk a mile in her company. I never see my mother walk unless it is between stores at the mall or along Michigan Avenue as she heads to Bloomingdale's. In fact, we scatter some of her ashes outside of the store. She never swims or plays golf. It isn't that she's agoraphobic, because supermarkets, the hairdresser, department stores are never a problem. It's more as if my mother doesn't like the natural world.

I prod her on vacations to put her feet in the ocean, to dip into the pool. I ask her to come with me to feed some ducks. She says she is allergic to the sun. Once, when I'm much older, I ask what happens to her in the sun. "I get freckles," she replies.

Sometimes I use her vanity table. It is, after all, in my room. I like to sit there and brush my hair. I try on her lipstick. Dab on a little of her perfume. I'm sitting at her vanity brushing my hair when she comes in to tell me that my best friend Tommy has died of bone cancer. I'm in third grade. In second grade Tommy taught me how to tie my shoes. Because I'm left-handed, it was difficult for me to learn. Sometimes, if we were late for recess, he just tied them for me. She stands in the doorway. "Tommy's dead," she tells me. "It's a blessing." Then she comes up behind me, takes the brush, and finishes brushing my hair.

89

India, 2011

THAT NIGHT I eat in my room. I have a fever and all I want is soup. I miss Larry. The feeling is visceral. His body is warm and mine is cold. There is a rhythm to our days. A morning walk with the dog, a glass of wine for me and a beer for him at the end of the day. Chats about bills to pay, tasks to perform. Who takes care of what. We work together as a well-oiled machine. But what we really do well is talk. We can talk for hours: about our daughter, about what it means to be a writer, about the state of the world. André Malraux wrote that a happy marriage is a long conversation that ends too soon. I just want it to go on and on.

What time is it in New York? Can I call my husband? It is too early to Skype. And he probably won't pick up anyway. Outside, the moon illumines the fields where the flowers and vegetables have all frozen on their stalks and vines. I press my lips to the window, and it is cold.

90

THREE DECADES AGO, I'm a single parent, living in Laguna Beach, California. I have a job and I'm trying to make a go of it, but my daughter isn't even a year old and my partner of many years hasn't wanted to make it "legal." He's back East, as are the rest of my family and friends. Essentially, I'm on my own. It wasn't really my decision to leave New York and move to California. I had a teaching job that ended, and one was offered to me out West. So I thought, Why not? Wasn't California the place of fresh starts?

Now I'm not so sure. I've been there for almost two months and things aren't going my way. There are rumors of a mountain lion in the hills above my house. My neighbors have a cat that uses the sandbox as its litter box. Ramona, the nanny I've hired, burns pots and hides them while I'm at work in places where she thinks I won't look. And Kate rarely sleeps. When I discuss this with her pediatrician, the aptly named Dr. Softness, he tells me to put her in her crib and just leave her there. Instead I take her on long car rides into the desert during which she sleeps, but she wakes up as soon as we get home. On the weekends I feel as if I've fallen off a cliff. I take care of Kate, try to grade papers during the rare times when she sleeps, or plug her into *Dumbo*, which she watches endlessly. Her favorite activity is the drive-through car wash and I have the cleanest car in Southern California.

One night, completely exhausted, I tumble into bed and have this dream. I dream that I have gone to Richmond, Virginia (a place I'd never been), and that Richard (my daughter's biological father) is coming to kidnap her. He's going to take her across the border into Canada and I'll never see her again. In the dream I'm desperately seeking someone who can stop him at the border. I wake, terrified and trembling. It's Sunday and I have another long day ahead.

Time crawls on without much improvement. My job is a two-year commitment and I'm having difficulty making it through the first semester. Then one afternoon I get a call from an old acquaintance. He's running a workshop at Virginia Commonwealth University and asks me if I'd like to spend two weeks in Richmond next summer. Kate's playing on the floor, inching toward an electric socket, but I stand, holding the phone, frozen in place. Is this some cosmic joke? My appointment in Samarra? Premonition or mere coincidence, my decision is clear. Something is sending me to Richmond.

I make it through the holidays and into the spring. I remain alone in a place where I have no family and few friends, a baby who won't sleep, and a job I can barely tolerate. It seems as if I can get no traction in my life. I'm writing in fits and starts. In search of a distraction, I begin hanging out with New Age groups. I attend UFO abductee support groups and channeling sessions with the extraterrestrial Ashtar and his intergalactic fleet. I fly as an angel in the Crystal Cathedral. I go to channeling sessions where a group of women determine that I haven't really given birth to my daughter. "So," I ask, "who is the babysitter watching back home?"

I date a bit from time to time. Blind dates, chance encounters. On the way to dinner one man comments that it's nice of me to allow the help to bring her child over. When I tell him it's my child, he says I betrayed him and refuses to pay for dinner. I give up dating. I give up hoping. I devote myself to my daughter and our lives together as best I can. Anyway, I have so much to do, I don't have time to think about the future. And for a while I don't think about that dream.

Then summer rolls around and it's at last time to meet my maker, my destiny, or whatever has called me to Richmond. My mother, with whom I have made relative peace, has agreed to take care of Kate for the first week of the conference. She'll join me along with my thirteen-year-old nephew and Kate for the second week. I'm given an apartment in the Gladding Residence Center. This is where, I'm told, visiting athletes stay. It's a dormitory of cinder-block walls. A rocking chair for Kate has been placed in the middle of the room.

At the Gladding Residence Center there's only one other attendee. (In fact, it turns out that he and I are the only attendees who aren't local.) A young, good-looking (if I'd been looking) man named Larry. He's supposed to be in another workshop but for whatever reason the director moves him into mine. On our second day I'm in the cafeteria, grabbing lunch, and I see Larry in line behind me. He smiles and waves. He has a nice smile and bright blue eyes. A thoughtful, caring face. But I'm in no shape to socialize. I'm barely getting through the day. But another student who's sitting in the cafeteria waves us over, and so Larry and I wind up having lunch together.

"So what did you do this morning?" the other student asks us. I tell them that I'd read papers and written critiques of their work. Then Larry informs us that he's taken the walking tour of old Richmond. He tells us about the architecture and the interesting historical insights he's gleaned from the tour and I think to myself, "What a nice thing. A man who takes himself on a walking tour."

"I'd like to do something like that," I tell him. "Are there any more tours?"

"Well," Larry said with a laugh, "there is a slavery exhibit at the local historical society."

A slavery exhibit? Larry shrugs. It seems like a grim and perhaps ominous first date, but we agree to go and see it the following afternoon. The slavery exhibit is predictably awful, and somehow we bond over the bizarreness of the concept, and then return to the Gladding Residence Center, where without notice they've closed the cafeteria for the rest of the summer.

"So," Larry says, "do you want to have dinner? There's a nice tearoom nearby. I think it has Southern cooking." I tell him that I can't because I have papers to grade, and I have to do my laundry. "I could do your laundry," he says.

"You want to do my laundry?"

"Well, I have to do mine . . ."

I pause momentarily to wonder if there isn't something creepy about this. Since Kate was born, I have taken care of her. No one has taken care of me. No one has offered. So I give Larry my laundry bag and, two hours later, he returns it, even my underwear warm and folded. That evening we go to Morton's Tea Room, where we eat the best fried chicken I've ever had. Over dinner I think to myself, "Is this the moment when I tell him that I have an eighteen-month-old child, or should I just enjoy myself for another day or so?"

The next night, since there's nowhere to eat near the

residence center, we have dinner again. I mean to tell him over dinner, but he asks if I want to see a movie. *Bull Durham* is playing nearby. It's blistering hot as we ride to the movies, my feet on the dashboard. We watch the movie, laughing, enjoying ourselves. And I still haven't told him about the baby. And I'm starting to like him. I'm enjoying his company. He's easy to be with. After the movie as we walk back to his car, I notice the motto on his license plates: "Yours to Discover." And then I notice the plates themselves.

"You're from Ontario?" I ask.

"Yes, actually I'm teaching in a place called North Bay."

Slowly the dream is coming back to me and it doesn't seem possible, but here it is. "So, you're Canadian?"

And yes, he is.

By the next night we're spending all of our time together and it's clear to me that things are starting to matter. I know I have to tell him and then listen as he makes pleasant excuses about wanting a family of his own or not being ready for responsibility. And that will be that. Over dinner I say, "I have something to tell you . . . It's really important." He nods, looking concerned. "On Saturday my mother, my nephew, and . . ." Deep sigh because I know what's coming. He's about to hightail it to the hills. "My baby daughter are arriving."

Larry listens, cocking his head. "That's it? You aren't married or sick or something?"

"No." I laugh. "Why?"

"I was worried that something was wrong." He smiles. "So what time do we have to pick them up?"

A few weeks later I leave California and move back to New York. And soon Larry is flying down from Canada every weekend and Kate is starting to call him Daddy. And I know this can't go on. When I call to tell him I want to break up, he tells me that he's moving to New York. "It's not going to work from here," he says.

"All right," I reply, "but I don't want to live together. I'm just not ready. And I have to think of Kate . . ." I don't want her to grow attached to a man who isn't going to stay in her life. Larry asks if I'll help him find an apartment and I say that I will.

The next day my upstairs neighbor knocks on my door. She's a professional mime and clown and she has just returned from a tour of Eastern Europe, where she's done street theater. She's going on about a Polish boat mechanic she met in Gdańsk and how it was love at first sight except that she doesn't speak Polish and he doesn't speak English. It's a long, rambling monologue but finally she gets to the point. She's going to move to Poland to learn the language and do I know anyone who might want to sublet her apartment?

And I tell her I do.

91

TIGERS WERE VIRTUALLY UNKNOWN in Europe for centuries. In Aristotle's *History of Animals*, he makes no mention of the tiger. The first known tiger to visit Europe came via one of Alexander the Great's faithful generals, who brought one to Athens in 323 BC and displayed this beast, once believed to be a myth, in front of the Acropolis for all to see. Still the tiger remained an obscure and enigmatic beast. In *The Travels of Marco Polo*, Marco Polo describes how "the Great Khan has many leopards, which are good for hunting and the taking of beasts . . . He has several great lions, larger than those of Babylonia. They have very handsome coats, of beautiful color, striped lengthwise with black, red, and white."

Of course, these red-striped lions weren't lions at all. They were tigers. But only those who had crossed into Asia had seen them before.

92

"YOU WILL BE a restless wanderer." This was God's curse to Cain.

93

Brooklyn, 2009

ON A BLEAK NOVEMBER DAY I wake and look outside. The sky is gray. The oak tree in our yard is shedding the last of its leaves. Squirrels grow fat as they chomp on acorns, preparing for another winter. They scamper along the lines of cable that we refer to as "the squirrel highway." But on that gray morning, gazing outside, I'm bored. And, though I hate to admit it, in despair. I've gone almost nowhere in more than two years. And one year of that I spent laid up, often in bed.

Just the other day a former student wrote from Egypt, where he was traveling for three weeks. He shared with me that he put an Italian passport cover on his American passport in case of a terrorist attack. A clever precaution, I thought. A close friend, heading to India, asked me to come over and help her pack. "You're such a good packer," she said. A good packer? This had never been how I defined myself. It was not how I wanted my friends to remember me.

A friend on Facebook shares a picture of a monastery, perched on a pinnacle of a rock, in Bhutan. It's called the Tiger's Nest because it looks unattainable. I sit, staring at the picture, longing to go, but I'm sure I can't hike a mile, let alone up to a place in the heavens. Since my accident I've hardly traveled and certainly not solo. For months I've been stuck at home as if a locked door stood between me and the world. In a way I suppose it does.

It's been almost two years since my accident. I had a second surgery to remove the metal plate, but walking remains painful, my balance unsure. I can no longer walk on a beach. Within moments the uneven sand causes my ankle to swell. I can't hike. I have to be very careful what shoes I wear. It is only recently that I gave up walking with a cane—and that was because I left it in a cab. Something that I took as a good sign at the time but that really just meant I forgot my cane.

Now I'm suffering from travel envy. Some people covet riches or another person's good looks. I covet journeys. Friends who tell me they are off to Bali, hiking in Machu Picchu, camel trekking along the Nile. But my friend asking me to help her pack is the last straw. I have no plans. No maps or brochures lie scattered around the house as they often do. "Oh," my mother used to say, "she's looking at maps." That was a sure sign I'd soon be on my way. I couldn't stay in one place for long.

But it has been a while since my dog-eared atlas that still has Yugoslavia and the Soviet Union in its pages has left the shelf. The plastic bin where I keep maps is gathering dust. Maps. I collect them. I have for years. I keep them all in this bin. From time to time I like to take them out, retrace the steps I've taken through Prague or Kyoto. I've spent much of the past thirty years on the road, wandering through Latin America, traversing the Gobi desert. But in the last two years I've spent my time wanting to travel and hardly being able to. I've spent more time than I'd ever imagined at home. "Stuck" would be the operative word. As another squirrel scurries by, I turn to Larry, who is waking up. "I need to get away."

He looks at me, nodding. He knows what I've been through. What we've both been through. This doesn't surprise him. It is as if he expected it. "Where do you want to go?" he asks, groggy from sleep.

"Everywhere," I tell him. In truth I don't care. I want to go everywhere.

94

Brooklyn, 2010

AN INVITATION ARRIVES. It comes in an embossed envelope that contains all of our names. We are invited to attend the Hindu wedding of Kate's best friend's cousin. The wedding is to be held in Lucknow, India, on June 13, 2010, which a soothsayer has declared to be a propitious date. When I give Kate the invitation, she says she's going. As a college graduation present we promised her an airplane ticket. And she wants one to Mumbai. And so do I.

For days I hem and haw. We could go together. I envision us, wrapped in saris, red bindis on our foreheads for the wedding, then pushing on into the hills of Bengal.

Finally I gather the strength to ask, though I already sense what the answer will be, but still I hope against hope. At last I come out with it. "The invitation is really for all of us, isn't it?" I say.

But Kate shakes her head. "I'm doing this on my own," she replies. I cannot ignore the finality in her tone. A few weeks later as I am about to begin a new round of physical therapy, my suitcase leaves without me. Kate has packed it with lightweight linens, including all of my yoga pants, because the temperature the previous week in Lucknow was 108. On the day her plane lands in Mumbai a rubber slide of the *Titanic* is being blown up in front of my house. It is our annual block party, and for the rest of the day I watch children sliding from the sinking ship into a wading pool.

Days later I receive an e-mail from Kate in Mumbai. They have picked out the gold-and-emerald sari for the wedding. And she has accompanied the groom's family to the temple for prayer. She was asked to join them in their holiest of ceremonies and she put her hands with theirs into the flame. This is a great honor. For the wedding she will be swathed in silk. She will have a bindi on her forehead to mark the third eye of wisdom. Then she asks me to tell her what is happening at home. What can I say? We moved two planters into the back of the garden. I have scheduled dental appointments for all. What I can't tell her is this: I long to put my hands in the fire. I want to burn.

95

BORGES WRITES, "Time is the substance I am made of. Time is a river which sweeps me along, but I am the river; it is a tiger which destroys me, but I am the tiger; it is a fire which consumes me, but I am the fire."

96

India, 2011

VIBHAV IS AS CHEERFUL as Ajay was glum. And while Ajay was contemplative, Vibhav is all about chatter. From the moment I get into the jeep until he drops me off back at the hotel he's just chattering away. He must think it is his job to keep me entertained but it only makes me burrow deeper into myself. I miss Ajay with his quiet manner and Sudhir with his eccentric mustache and weird love of snakes.

We come upon a savanna that is filled with spotted deer. Ears perked, eyes alert, they are ready to run in a heartbeat. Except for a few instances in the ocean and perhaps now, I've never had the experience of not being at the top of the food chain. But the deer clearly know that, at any moment, they can be eaten. Their perked ears, always moving, their darting eyes, attest to this fact. No one eats the tiger—except the Chinese who believe the blood and bones contain special powers. And a few poachers I've read about who say that tiger meat is sweet and juicy like chicken.

The only natural enemy that the tiger has is man. Here in Kahna there are twenty-one thousand spotted deer, and the spotted deer make up 52 percent of the tiger's diet. No wonder their ears are twitching. We pause at the savanna, then keep driving around. My driver and guide hear the alarm calls of peacocks, monkeys, wild chickens, spotted deer, barking deer, sambar deer (while I, of course, hear nothing at all), but after hours of driving on the rutted roads, still no sign of the tiger.

Then suddenly in the late afternoon we hear something. We all hear it. Even me. It sounds like an engine revving up, but it is in fact a growl. A real tiger's growl. It starts low, but then it ripples through the jungle until it is a full-fledged roar. All around us we hear the alarm calls of peacocks and deer. Ahead of us the dust of a speeding jeep recedes down the road, and we set out after it. We race around the bends and I'm holding on to the frame of the jeep, scanning the woods for some sign of a six-hundred-pound striped animal. We follow the wake of the other jeep until it leads us to a dry riverbed where drivers and guides are all pointing at the ground.

There on the path, heading toward a pond, I see them. Pugmarks. Fresh pugmarks. I see them in the ground by the banks of the river. A male tiger has walked through here less than an hour ago. Vibhav knows it is a male because of the circular mark. The female's is oval. No one knows why, but this is so. It is just one more mystery to be solved. The tiger crossed this riverbed just moments ago, but now he's gone. Our eyes scan the low-lying scrub, the edges of the river, but he could be anywhere.

As we drive back to the hotel, the tiger and its pug-mark have morphed into "she." *All tigers you cannot see are she.* Ajay's words echo in my head. That apex predator, fierce and ferocious. Admired for her fearful symmetry. A solitary creature who succeeds in only a third of her kills. Who will mate for a day, then go on her lonely way. But never get between the tigress and her cubs. And give her room to be wild and free. How can I not see the artist in her? How can she not see the tiger in me?

We ride along the bumpy road through the villages, and Vibhav is humming a song. His voice is soft and melodious, and when he stops, I ask him what he was singing. It is a poem of the great Indian writer Rabindranath Tagore that has been set to music. Vibhav translates it for me. "I am in a boat moored to a dock. This is a waste of time. My morning is wasted. Everything is wasted. I am going to cut the tether. I am going to move out. I will not be afraid of the furrowed brow of the storm. I will make it my friend."

This is a song you sing, Vibhav explains, when you find yourself at a crossroads.

97

YOGI BERRA FAMOUSLY SAID, "When you come to the fork in the road, take it."

98

THE TALMUD SAYS that when you must choose between two things and you cannot decide, choose the third. Remember that for Yann Martel the tiger was his third choice.

99

IT IS 1974 and I'm living in New York. I've begun a graduate program at Columbia in comparative literature because I think, eventually, I can earn a living, but in truth I have no idea what I want. I've considered law school, film school. The dream of being a writer eludes me. Yet I'm writing all the time, scribbling poems and stories, notes for a novel. Meanwhile I'm living in a dorm, International House. The woman across the hall from me, named Marcia, plays her music way too loud. One afternoon I knock on her door and ask Marcia to turn her music down, and she screams at me. She calls me names, and I find myself paralyzed before her rage. The next day I move to a "quiet hall."

A few weeks later a Pakistani poet named Shuja tells me over dinner that he's organizing a poetry reading and asks me to read. I tell him that I'm not a writer, but he won't take no for an answer. "You're studying comparative literature. You must also be writing."

Of course, I'm writing. Much more than I'm studying, in fact. But I've never shared my work with anyone. Once in high school I showed my friend Phyllis a poem and she said it was "nice." That was the one and only time I've shared my work. That is, until Shuja insists that I show him my poems. I have no idea how he talks me into it, but one evening he comes to my room and I literally open the drawer. For the better part of an hour Shuja leafs through the sheaves of papers that I've stuffed in there. He shuffles pages, putting them in piles. After a time, he turns to me and says, "You are a very good third-rate poet."

And I wonder why I opened my drawer for someone to tell me this.

But he goes on: "Shakespeare was a first-rate poet. John Donne was a second-rate poet. Anne Sexton is a third-rate poet." Well, if Anne Sexton is third-rate, I could live with that. One of the piles Shuja has arranged contains five of my poems. "Here," he says, "you will read these." And for some reason I agree.

On the evening of the event I walk into a packed room and there, sitting in the front row, right in front of the podium, is my nemesis, Marcia. I feel as if I could read in front of anyone but her. But it's too late. The reading proceeds. I'm trembling as I read my poems. In fact I think I will faint. Afterward Marcia comes up to me and says, "If I'd known you were writing those poems, I would have kept my music down."

Marcia tells me to send my poems to *The Columbia Review*. And when they accept them, I knock on Marcia's door with flowers to thank her. Years later when I am a writer and giving readings, I will at times catch a glimpse of Marcia in the audience.

That spring I drop out of graduate school. I have completed five language exams, all of my written and oral exams. All I have to do is write a thesis. When I walk away, my adviser never speaks to me again.

100

A COURTIER falls in love with a princess and her barbaric father makes him submit to a test he has devised for criminals. In an arena there are two doors. Behind one is a tiger that will devour him. Behind the other is a beautiful woman whom he must marry—though it is not the princess he loves. The princess knows which door houses the tiger and which the other woman. She also knows that her beloved will either be devoured by the tiger or be forced to marry another woman.

Just before he must decide, the courtier looks at his beloved and she gives him a nod toward one of the doors. But the story stops here. We never learn the courtier's fate. The problem is unsolvable, the choice impossible.

101

PICO IYER WRITES: "We travel, initially, to lose ourselves, and we travel, next, to find ourselves. We travel to open our hearts and eyes . . . And we travel, in essence, to become young fools again—to slow time down, get taken in and fall in love once more." To become young fools, to slow time down. Isn't that what we are all looking for? To return to beginnings. The first day of kindergarten and my mother has to pry my fingers from her hand. I won't let go. When she manages to pull away, I sob into the skirts of Miss Malvey. I don't know how long I cry, but when I stop and look around the first thing I see is a large map of an empty city on the floor and a boy who is putting buildings, houses, trees, and cars into the city. I get on the floor and join him. His name is Paul and he's happy to share. I begin making a city of my own. I make it over and over again. It is never the same place. I never want it to be.

Soon I am able to walk to and from school every day. I walk home. I forge my way slowly into the world. Into my own city of unknown streets, other people's houses, all waiting to be explored.

102

"THE STORY OF CATS is a story of meat," Elizabeth Marshall Thomas writes in her amazing book *The Tribe of Tiger*.

Thomas explains how mammals essentially descended from two branches: the Vulpavines, or the Fox Tribe, and the Viverravines, the Mongoose Tribe. During the Oligocene epoch, members of the Fox Tribe began to evolve into bears, raccoons, weasels, and wolves. Members of the Mongoose Tribe became mongoose, hyenas, and cats.

The cats evolved as full-fledged carnivores. While other mammals diversified their diets, the cats did not. Not only did they not diversify their diets to include plants and fruits, but their diets also don't include carrion. Cats became what is known as obligate carnivores. That is, they have no choice. Tigers are almost entirely dependent on captured animal protein for their diet and, as Thomas points out, their modus operandi is lurk and leap. Basically, a tiger is either eating or hunting. Most old tigers die of starvation because they can no longer succeed in their kills.

103

India, 2011

I HAVE MORE OR LESS GIVEN UP on seeing a tiger in the wild. The cold is keeping them away. I am ready to admit defeat. "So," I say to Vibhav as we leave the jungle on the second day, "I guess I'm not going to see a tiger after all."

"Oh, you can see one. You will. I can guarantee it."

Guarantee it? I have heard this before, of course. "But perhaps you must do elephant walk."

"Elephant walk? What is that?"

Vibhav explains that in the early morning the mahouts go out into the jungle and find a place where a tiger lies. Somehow, they know where to look. Then they let the guides know where to come. If I'm going to see a tiger in the wild this might be my last chance. I don't really want to do elephant walk. It is a practice that I'm sure is frowned upon by conservationists. One naturalist will later tell me that it is a "disaster" for tourists to be going into the bush on elephants, looking for tigers.

And it isn't great for the elephants either. Tigers have been known to rip out the eyes of elephants who startle them in the bush or come upon them when they're with a kill. But tomorrow will be my eighth and final safari. I've been with Ajay, one of the best jungle guides in all of India, and now Vibhav, for almost two weeks and no tiger. Short of hanging a lot of bed linen throughout the jungle, I've given up on finding a tiger just by driving around and listening for alarm calls.

We stop at a crossroads and Sonu stands up. He is listening. His eyes dart about. Like Ajay, this young man has grown up in this place and he hears things I cannot imagine. Then he points into the distance. "Sambar deer alarm call," he says.

I know now to sit down and hold on as Sonu dashes ahead. He zips around turns, avoids ruts, makes a wide turn, until suddenly we come to a clearing. Here we stop, and again silence. Nothing. I wait, but I don't see a thing. Suddenly Vibhav grabs my hand. "There," he whispers, pointing.

Still I see nothing. In the distance the bushes seem to rustle, but that is all. Vibhav shrugs. Whatever it was— the wind, a lost fawn—the movement stops, and we push on. This is not, after all, an expedition. I'm not searching for the snow leopard in the Himalayas or the elusive, and probably extinct, ivory-billed woodpecker in a bayou outside of Baton Rouge. I am just on the tourist trail, a bumpy and unused trail though it may be. Still, the afternoon ends, once more, without the sighting of a tiger.

104

IN *Invisible Cities*, Italo Calvino writes: "You walk for days among trees and among stones. Rarely does the eye light on a thing, and then only when it has recognized that thing as the sign of another thing: a print in the sand indicates the tiger's passage; a marsh announces a vein of water; the hibiscus flower, the end of winter. All the rest is silent and interchangeable; trees and stones are only what they are." As Calvino understands, and I understand now, the thing itself eludes us. Reach for the stars, my father always said, even though you'll never touch them. The journey is everything.

105

India, 2011

IN THE MORNING an elephant is waiting for me. As it is also waiting for the four other jeep-loads of tourists who are ahead of me in line. Young children, old women, fat men are prodded up a ladder onto the old elephant's back. They disappear for a few minutes, then return with faint grins on their faces. It appears that they have seen something. At last it is my turn and, I assume because I am solo in my jeep (again), I am solo, except for the mahout, on my elephant as well. Once I am topside it is what I imagine it must be like to ride shotgun in a Sherman tank as you lurch into enemy territory.

Suddenly the mahout kicks my poor beast and clobbers it on the head with his stick and the elephant lumbers into the dense bush. I ride for about five minutes when the mahout starts kicking the elephant again around the ears with his heels. The elephant backs up, then comes to a halt. With his long stick the mahout pulls back some branches. Then he starts frantically kicking his elephant again, shouting at me—something I can't quite understand and then I do. "Tiger, tiger."

I'm not sure what I was expecting. I was hoping for at least a moment of what Konrad Lorenz, the famed Austrian zoologist, called the *heiliger schauer*, "the Holy Shiver," the terror that predators inspire in their prey. And the tiger, after all, is an apex predator. He is at the top of his food chain and here, in his jungle, I am not. So I was hoping at least for a look, a gaze, its green eyes set on me for an instant so I could experience, albeit from an elephant's back, what it means when a tiger has you in its sights.

Instead, as the bushes open, there is, taking a snooze, well, a tiger. She is big and she is wild, but she also seems quite content to doze with elephants tramping around her and a bunch of tourists shooting film. It is as if she was sent by central casting (and in a way she was). I so wanted to have a different kind of moment and in truth I wanted to share it with Ajay and Sudhir. I wanted a tiger to walk out of the jungle on its way to devour some poor spotted deer and for an instant lock eyes with me. So I've traveled halfway around the world to see a tiger who is, more or less, a tourist attraction, taking a nap.

A few moments later the elephant turns, and we amble back to the road, my tiger now behind me. Can this be it? Is this all? Have I journeyed so far for so little? Back where the jeep awaits, I climb off the elephant, feeling dismayed. It is that let-down feeling when you finish a book you've loved with an unsatisfying ending. There is time left and Vibhav, perhaps sensing my disappointment, suggests we drive around for a bit. "I will tell you a funny story," he says. It seems that this young tigress whom we've just seen likes to do the elephant walk. She's not very shy and she seems to enjoy the attention. "Her mother," he tells me, "was the same way. She always came out for elephant walk." So it's kind of a family concession, I guess, but still . . . I wish it were different. This was hardly seeing a tiger in the wild.

We come off a ridge, driving toward a ravine, and are about to circle back when Vibhav begins to point frantically. He taps Sonu on the shoulder and immediately Sonu brings the jeep to a halt, then begins to back up. "Look." He's pointing. Deep in a ravine the bushes are moving, and whatever is making them move is coming closer to me. The tigress is now walking. I catch a glimpse of her. I can make out her stripes.

And there she is. She is large and sleek and moves like a well-oiled machine. Orange and black. Just as I'd envisioned her. I stand up, gripping the frame of the jeep, when she jumps onto the road, not twenty feet from me. She pauses, as if deciding which way to go, and then yawns. As she looks around, I gaze into her amber eyes. We stare at each other, and there it is. A creature truly wild, truly free. No longer hidden, she stands in the middle of the road, brilliant in all her glory. Then she gives a long feline stretch, crosses the road on her white fluffy paws that could, with a single swat, break a person's neck. She slips down into the brush on the other side. Behind the ridge she disappears. The bushes rustle as she descends into the forest. I watch her go as I stand, staring until the movement stops and she has moved back into the dense jungle from where she emerged and where she belongs.

Then it is time to leave. As we approach the gate to

Kahna, Vibhav turns to me. For once he is serious. "So you found your tiger, Mary, didn't you?"

I nod, smiling. "Yes, I did."

We drive out of the park in silence. Just before the main road a family of deer, including a very young fawn, appears. Overhead, monkeys nibble on leaves and suddenly a wild boar leaps out of the bushes and crosses the road. I shake my head. "This is so beautiful," I say. For the rest of the ride no one says a thing.

106

TO SEE A TIGER in your dream represents power and your ability to exert it in various situations. The dream may also indicate that you need to take more of a leadership role. Alternatively, the tiger represents female sexuality, aggression, and seduction.

To dream that you are attacked by a tiger refers to the emotions that you have repressed because you were afraid of confronting them.

To see a caged tiger in your dream suggests that your repressed feelings are on the verge of surfacing.

107

India, 2011

AT THE TRAIN STATION in Nagpur a man with his legs twisted in unimaginable ways drags himself along the ground with one hand. He looks as if someone neatly folded him and he spent his life in a drawer. Another man with broken twigs for legs and a bag of rice on his back hobbles by. It is close to ten as Dinesh and I pull into the parking lot of this huge, dark, dusty station that boils with a cauldron of humanity.

He will leave me here as I push on to Mumbai, which I've decided to travel to by train. But I'm having second thoughts. Women wrapped in scarves drag crying children. Old men and women cling to one another's arms. A girl without hands holds a begging cup in the stumps of her arms. Inside the station the floor is covered in blankets upon which are sitting or lying down turbaned old men, women in saris, shawls around their arms, half-naked children, snot running down their noses. Two bodies lie in the middle of the floor, wrapped in white sheets. I assume they are dead until I see a large water bottle tucked between their heads. Dead people don't drink water.

I feel as if I have fallen into a painting by Bruegel. The one with all the souls, battling in hell. Out on the platform I huddle with a family, wrapped in blankets and scarves. We are all shivering, watching as dreary train after dreary train passes by. Out of nowhere a line of barefoot holy men, dressed only in loincloths of various shades of orange, yellow, and saffron, carrying wooden staffs, marches past in silence, single file. At last a dingy green train with slats for windows pulls into the station. I stand on the platform as the cars roll by, labeled LUGGAGE, DISABLED, SECOND-CLASS SLEEPER #43.

I check the ticket I purchased back home. It is for the second-class sleeper and the car number is 43. Dinesh looks at my ticket and solemnly nods. I gaze at the dark, soiled windows, the slats for windows, hoping that somehow this isn't my train, but I cannot wait long because suddenly everyone is piling on—men hoisting their luggage, women with their shopping bags. I fling myself and my luggage up the stairs along with the rest of the shoving throng, with an assist from Dinesh, who waves at me from the platform. "Have a safe journey," he says as I fight my way into the car.

Inside, the car is lined in berths with a sackcloth curtain for privacy. Turbaned men, returning from a pilgrimage, lie in most of the beds. A woman is asleep in my berth. I don't know what to do, but the conductor shakes her. The woman looks up at me, groggily, then points across the aisle to an upper berth that amounts to a narrow, cramped shelf, and asks if I wouldn't mind sleeping there. It has no window and no light.

My claustrophobia kicks in. "I'm sorry," I tell her. "I'm not feeling well, and I just can't sleep up there." Disgruntled, she gets up, dragging her things with her. She leaves me her used linens to sleep on. As I crawl into bed, a cockroach is climbing the wall.

It is freezing on the train. I'm not sure when I've ever been this cold. Even Delhi and Pench seem warmer than this train—perhaps in part because the doorway between cars is open and my berth is just feet away. My cough has returned with a vengeance (not that it ever really left) and I'm hacking like crazy. At any moment I'm expecting to see blood. I begin to dig out every article of clothing in my wheelie or backpack that provides any warmth. I pull out a long-sleeve tee, a long-sleeve cotton shirt, my sweatshirt, jeans over yoga pants, three pairs of socks.

Still, I cannot get warm. I put on layer after layer, but I may as well be naked. My hot-water bottle lies in my suitcase as limp and lifeless as roadkill. I am coughing and my head throbs. I still have a few swallows of whiskey from the last bottle Dinesh purchased for me and I drink it until it is done. Somewhere in the compartment men speak in voices so loudly that it makes me think something is wrong. An argument, an accident. I peek out from behind my curtain and see that the conductor and four or five men are having tea in a bunk across from me. They are laughing, swapping stories. The fact that it is the middle of the night means nothing to them. They look at me, wondering what the matter might be. I shake my head and go back to my berth.

It is perhaps at this moment that I miss Larry the most.

But it will be days before I see him again. Before we can really have a talk. For years I traveled through Latin America, from Beijing to Berlin, down the Mississippi, and now to India. I sought out adventures and learned along the way that I could do this on my own. I know that I can. I also know that it is all right to have someone. And it is all right not to want to do this alone anymore. Now in my cold berth I long for warmth as I try to make it through the night.

Closing my eyes, I see my tigers. The one in my dreams, the ones I have searched for and never found, and the one that sprang out before me in the jungle. As I'm drifting off, I imagine her, moving stealthily in the bush, silent, hunting. Her amber eyes fixed on her prey. In my dreams those eyes turn blue. At last she and I are one and the same.

I sleep for a while, aware of the jerking of the train, then wake, colder than before.

Between cars the door is open, sending in a chilling draft, and I get up to close it. We are stopped at a station. It is about four in the morning, and on the platform the hungry and poor huddle, children cry beside their sleeping mothers. A bleating goat mills about. Women tug their shawls tightly around them while men in sandals and thin linen try to sleep, pressed against their bags of clothing and rice. Some stare straight ahead, trembling with the cold. They sit in a soupy fog. For the rest of the night and into the morning, all I see is this fog.

108

RECENTLY, while hiking in Nepal, a Dutch tourist and his guide were attacked by a tiger. The guide was slightly injured, fending off the tiger and giving the tourist enough time to climb a tree. The young man climbed six meters off the ground. For two hours he clung to the tree while the tiger paced below it. Tigers, it turns out, aren't very good at climbing trees. They are built to pounce, and most of their weight is forward. Their big thick front paws are intended to capture prey, not to cling to branches. But the young man did not know this as he waited to be rescued.

109

IN *Equus*, Peter Shaffer's play about a boy who blinds six horses, the psychiatrist says something that has stayed with me: "I can cure him of his madness, but I will take away his passion." I saw the play in New York many years ago when I first moved to the city, but it resonates for me to this day. There was a time when, perhaps, I was a bit on the wrong side of that equation, not mad but not entirely sane. I was also passionate about everything I did. Never mind the drugs, the booze, the one-night stands it took me to get there. I struggled to find the balance and now am not sure we ever can. Rilke, considering the prospect of psychoanalysis, said it this way: "If my devils are to leave me, I fear my angels will take flight as well."

How do we walk a thin line between sane and savage, between wild and tame? I think of all the jazz musicians, the brilliant poets and painters and actors who died young. Perhaps we cannot have it both ways, or perhaps we need to heed the words of Flaubert, who said, "Be regular and orderly in your life, so that you may be violent and original in your work."

Or circling back to Borges, "It is a tiger which destroys me, but I am the tiger."

110

India, 2011

BY THE TIME we pull into Mumbai I think my ears are going to explode. The pressure is unbearable. Naresh, a former colleague of my husband's, welcomes me to his house. It is a comfortable apartment with lots of windows. But I am too sick, it seems, to do almost anything. That night we head to a rooftop bar for a drink with his friends, but I bow out early. Naresh hails a rickshaw that runs me home.

The next day I wake up late, only feeling worse. My ears feel very strange. I can barely hear a thing. And I'm flying home in three days. Naresh has a deadline for a book on jazz in India, but he doesn't hesitate. "I'm taking you to see my family doctor." He is a swift walker and I follow him up and down streets until we come to a road of gardens where tomatoes and corn and squash grow. Toward the back of this road is an old house with a wide porch, filled with rocking chairs.

This is the doctor's waiting area. We sit on the porch, rocking, until she opens her door. Handing the previous patient a prescription, she greets Naresh with a big hug. She has been his doctor since he was a boy, and once she takes me in, she is very kind. She listens to my chest and checks my ears. "Your eustachian tubes are completely closed and you probably have an infection in your ears. You also have a very bad case of bronchitis. It is dangerous for you to fly, but in two or three days you will be better."

She writes me a prescription for drops and more medication, and Naresh, though he has so much work to do, takes me to the pharmacy and waits with me for my medicine. Then he walks me back to his place, where I lay my head over the side of the bed, as the doctor instructed, and put the drops in my nose, which go down my throat and make me gag. I rest and an hour later I am up, though not doing much better. Naresh has told me there's a bagel shop not far from his place and he suggests that I go there. "You just have to cross the main road, then go down about two streets to the right. You can't miss it."

There is nothing in this that puts me at ease. I am wary of the "you can't miss it" thing when spoken by a native. I love people who tell me that there's a mall or a café and if you just go a few miles one way, then make a right (or maybe it's a left) and keep going through a couple of traffic lights "you can't miss it." But you always do.

I decide to try to find the bagel shop. Walking to the end of Naresh's street, I pass large apartment buildings with names like Rendez-Vous, Pourquoi Pas, Cher Ami. All in French. I have no idea why. I pass two men sleeping on the sidewalk. Beside them is a cart with a large plastic bag from Bed Bath & Beyond, filled with their only belongings in this world. I walk around them, and then come to the intersection. I wait for the light (which really makes no difference), try to step out, and again I fail.

Since arriving in India I've been trying to cross the street. I can't say that things have improved. The learning curve appears to be steep. I've read somewhat that in India you should cross the road as if you are a sacred cow. That is, just walk into traffic and hope for the best.

But now, as vehicles careen past me from every which way, I know that I am not a sacred cow—not yet anyway. I pause for so long at the corner that two rickshaws stop to see if I want a ride.

Then a red street dog comes and stands next to me. I watch as the dog looks both ways, ventures out, dodges a few vehicles, ignores one or two screeching brakes, and makes it across. He looks back at me, then, it seems, waits. He is my guide. If a dog can do this, well, then I can, right? So I look the wrong way, and a rickshaw almost runs me down. I try again, stick out my hand like a native, and take a step. I walk into traffic as cars weave around me. I put up my hand as if I could really hold them back, but I keep going. And, to my surprise, some of them stop. I continue on step by step until at last I make it to the other side.

The dog disappears down a narrow street. I forget about the bagel shop and I follow. At first the street is lined with makeshift appliance stores, including one with a sign in the window that reads "I Fix Everything." Oh, if only he did. Open stands sell baubles and scarves. Others sell roti. I am hungry and think I'd like one but then think better of it. I'm returning home sick enough as it is. Catching one last glimpse of the dog's tail, I turn down another alleyway.

I find myself in a maze of tin-roofed shacks with burlap doors, blankets slung up as walls. People are lying on cardboard beside small fires upon which black pots steam. Men shave with knives in broken mirrors. The more I move within the slum the deeper I go. It is a labyrinth that seems almost without exit. Half-naked children flock to me, and I'm wishing I had something to give to them. I share the few cough drops that I have. I keep going with no idea which way to turn. Two bare-chested young men stop, and I say the name of the main street, the one I had left behind. They point in a direction that doesn't quite make sense, but it is possible I've gotten turned around.

A young woman appears behind a burlap door and she too points, indicating for me to make a left. Soon the whole neighborhood knows I am here and, as I dodge between blankets and shacks and steaming pots and naked children, I make my way. I am almost at my journey's end. I think of all I have done and seen in this past year. I have walked farther than Dr. Patel ever thought I would. Not without pain and stumbling, but still I have come so far.

And I have seen my tiger. Perhaps not the ferocious tiger of my dreams, but the flesh-and-blood tiger was never really the point, and I'm not sure I understood that until now. It was always about the journey, never the destination.

I think of my first trip to Europe with my mother. The highlights weren't the Colosseum or the Eiffel Tower, the Swiss guards or the Buckingham guards. They were my mother's first bite of peach melba at the Hotel de Vendôme, my stroll alone in the Borghese gardens, my mother's laughter as the bus driver greeted his two paramours, the shock on the waiter's face as she hurled her fake pearls into the sea. The truly important things happen in these moments. It is my mother who sent me on this journey. Not this trip to India but the one that has become my life. She has given me many things over the years—jewelry, china, silver. One day a few years ago she handed me her mink coat (which I have worn once). These things never meant much to me—perhaps because they meant so much to her.

I recall that first passport, holding it in my hands. I remember the moment the French customs official placed a stamp in its virgin pages and welcomed me to France. I cannot say that my mother and I have always had a smooth ride, but out of all that she has given me, or tried to give me, or pawn off on me, it is my passport and the world it opened up for me that has been the greatest gift.

My guides understood. I came to see everything. Yes, I saw a tiger. And a lot of other things. Now as I wander through this slum where strangers who have nothing are showing me the way, I recall a quote from Haruki Murakami: "What I was chasing in circles must have been the tail of the darkness inside of me." I think I've caught up with that tail at last.

111

TO THE TIGER WHO SLEEPS AT THE FOOT OF MY BED

(circa 1974)

Every night as I crawl into bed,
I have to be careful not to disturb
The tiger who sleeps at the foot of my bed.
He is a fat, yellow tiger with black stripes.
Three-inch canines, whiskers for radar
That detect my slightest move.
He is luminous as the alarm clock,
Glowing on the bed stand in the dark.
As I sleep, I must never rustle
The sheets or rise before he rises.
If he prowls, I close my eyes;
The prowler hates the voyeur.
Once when I was a child,
I kicked him in my sleep
And he rose from beneath the bed
And pounced on me as I lay on my back.
Since that night we've grown used to one another.

We've lived without mishap.

Always hungry, he lies
Curled at the foot of the bed,
Sharpening his claws on the posts,
And I am careful not to disturb him
For he has threatened to go away.

112

ON MY LAST AFTERNOON in India, I take a walk by the sea. I pass a spot where dozens of cars and pedestrians line up, seated in their cars or on a wall, all watching or waiting for something. That famous Bollywood star lives right across the street in a flat on the first floor, and he often appears and waves at the crowds. So they are waiting for a sighting. This man is known to beat his girlfriends. He is also the celebrity who one night, drunk, ran over four bakery workers who were sleeping on the sidewalk. He is out on bail. Still, the crowds huddle to see him.

The tide is out. Lovers, hand in hand, walk among the rocks. Some are even married, but they have no place to go. No privacy to be alone in their own homes so they come here to make love or just to talk. At times they forget themselves and some have been stranded as the tide comes in. Some have even drowned. Now when the tide comes in a bell rings to warn them and wake the lovers from their stupor.

Stray dogs, homeless children, and urinating men greet

me. Memorial benches line the sea walk. In memory of a mother, a father, a friend, a child. And one just reads GOD IS GREAT.

That night I'm in a car, leaving India, heading home. The cab has picked me up an hour and a half before I have to be at the airport (which is two hours before my flight). I am assuming that this is plenty of time. I am moving through a world of advanced skin-care treatments, Vodafone, ATMs, and jewelry shops with armed guards in front of them. We drive on, but soon we are stuck in a kind of market of saris, socks, cell phones, clock shops, sweetshops, chai stands, place mats, floral arrangements, ceramics, natural cleansing juices, dried fruits, seeds, milk, gold filigree, chemists, Cozy Corner coffee shops, caps, silicon pillow stuffing, fleece jackets, sexy underwear and teddies, Hindu gods, spices, nuts, vacuum cleaners, lightbulbs, banana leaves with something in them, fried bread, blue jeans, a miasma of pedestrians, double-decker buses, scooters, rickshaws, taxis, SUVs, a Hindu processional that includes drummers marching through the streets, all clambering under the "bye pass" [sic] which is also the main road to the airport.

We are stuck in an immense traffic jam. Motionless. We don't move for ten, fifteen minutes amid this froth of life. Suddenly to my left two boys, wearing illuminated red devil horns, start banging on the car window. They make faces, pointing at their horns, which flash on and off. To my right a girl who cannot be more than four or five pounds on the window as well, begging for alms. She presses her sobbing, snotty face to the glass and points to her brother, a boy of no more than two who lies shrieking on the median strip of the road. On the one side are the devils; on the other this begging child. Rolling down the window, to my driver's dismay, I slip her whatever rupees I can spare. The devils recede, taunting me. The child drifts away, her palm print still on the glass.

For forty minutes or so we don't move. An old impatience rises within me. I am still, after all—and will always be—my parents' child. Impatient, irritable. "Quite contrary," as my mother liked to say. How can I possibly make this plane? I badger the driver until he diverts and races down narrow roadways, past huts made out of cardboard and tin, until we are on the "highway" whose service area is lined with tents and their residents cooking, eating, shitting, chatting, bathing, begging, staring, sleeping, rocking their children to sleep. Just the mad stream of life forever going on.

Perhaps now I see the secret gift. For a while I stopped. I was afraid. I didn't know if I could go on. And if I could go it alone. Whether I would take another step or remain immobile, I was stuck wherever I was. Now something besides my ankle has healed. It seems as if I've been chasing my own tail. But some of that darkness has lifted. The demons have dropped back. I don't know what lies ahead, but I know I'm not afraid anymore. I am filled with gratitude. And, yes, in fact I have been lucky.

I am shaken by this fragile world. It is so easy to break and be broken. It is much harder to mend. There, sitting in traffic, between the devil and those motherless babes, I cannot know what I know now. I will make my flight. I will get well from whatever sickness is stuck inside my chest. My ankle will get stronger and carry me on, though never as it had before all this began. I will never run again and probably never skate again and I will always be unsteady and in some pain, but I can keep walking. I can go on.

Suddenly on the other side of the road, a pure white horse appears. It pulls a cart painted in brilliant colors and decorated with wreaths of flowers and tinsel, upon which a bride or god might sit. Shiva himself, that god of destruction and birth and renewal, might perch upon this cart. None of this makes sense. Yet everything is clear. In the night amid the jam of trucks and rickshaws and motorcycles and pedestrians, as I am close to missing my flight, this pale creature, like a vision from another world, gallops by.

AFTERWORD

IT HAS BEEN a dozen years since my accident and almost a decade since I traveled to India. In these years, the tiger, especially in India, has seen a strong resurgence in the wild, thanks to strenuous conservation efforts that include anti-poaching campaigns, creating new buffer zones and tiger reserves, and moving villages when need be (this remains a controversial practice). Through education and a focus on responsible tourism, India has made tremendous progress. A recent counting has estimated that there are approximately three thousand Bengal tigers in the wild, a 33 percent increase since 2014, when the last tiger counting was completed.

At the same time, a billion and a half people cohabitating with an apex predator that needs huge territory hasn't been that easy. The struggle continues between beast and man. Recently, angry villagers savagely killed a tiger that had attacked people, and a video of this killing went viral. And a tigress who had killed many people had to be hunted and killed when relocating her failed.

Yet clearly there is progress. Zoos and circuses such as SeaWorld are cutting back and/or eliminating their animal acts. Through good wildlife management, poaching is down. Yet the Chinese still believe that tiger bones and tiger blood will make them potent. They breed tigers for this purpose as well as trapping them in the wild. And hunters continue to want trophies. There are places in the United States where for a sizeable sum you can go on "safari" and shoot tigers.

Still, I am hopeful. The numbers are encouraging, and progress is being made. I am less optimistic about tigers in other parts of Asia, especially Sumatra and Malaysia, where there are only approximately another thousand left in the wild. For a greater understanding of tigers in general and the Amur, or Siberian, tiger in particular, I highly recommend John Valliant's outstanding book *The Tiger*.

And on a personal note, I am long past the point when the doctor who gave me his second opinion said I'd need an ankle replacement. Though, as I expected, I've never skated again, I walk miles every day. As long as I am able, I will never stop.

ACKNOWLEDGMENTS

First I must begin by thanking my incredible guides in India—Ajay Bahare and Vibhav Srivastava—and my drivers Dinesh, Sudhir, and Sonu. This book wouldn't have been possible without their help and, beyond that, their dedication to wildlife. The readers who helped me along the way were amazing. Thanks go to Dani Shapiro and Caroline Leavitt for their advice and enthusiasm, Barbara Grossman (who perhaps loved this book before I did), and Marc Kaufman, who read this when I was in need of his quick critical eye and did it in a day and discussed it with me in great detail. To my friend Maria Friedrich, who told me that I would one day see the silver lining, and to Naresh Fernandes, who gave me shelter and kindness in Mumbai. And to my doctor and his staff (whose names I have had to change here), whose professionalism and caring enabled me to heal and move on.

To my amazing editor Nan Talese, who is pretty ferocious herself and who has stuck with me for more than thirty years, and to the terrific staff at Knopf Doubleday, including Nan's assistant Carolyn Williams. I want to thank my wonderful agent, Ellen Levine, who has stood by me since day one, and her assistant, Martha Wydysh.

Thank you to my daughter, Kate, and her husband, Chris, whose love and support mean the world. And, as always, thanks to my partner, husband, fellow journeyman, best friend, first reader, finest critic, who, as always, read every word with patience and care and talked me through this book—and all the others—every step of the way. Without Larry nothing would be.

And finally I want to thank all those who work for the conservation of these extraordinary creatures in the wild—and all creatures who are at risk. It is my deepest hope that we find a way to keep the world wild and give these animals the room they need and the respect they deserve.